The Book of God's Promises

D0805046

THE
BOOK
of God's
Promises

TYNDALE HOUSE PUBLISHERS, INC.
WHEATON, ILLINOIS

Visit Tyndale's exciting Web site at www.tyndale.com

For fun Bible games and up-to-date information about *The Book,* visit
www.ireadthebook.com

ISBN 0-8423-3486-6

Printed in the United States of America

05 04 03 02 01 00 99
10 9   8   7   6   5   4   3   2   1

Preface

"Give your burdens to the Lord, and he will take care of you," says Psalm 55:22. A lovely promise, isn't it? The verse does not even specify that we bring "life-threatening" or "major" burdens to the Lord. We can bring *any* of them—great or small, physical or emotional or spiritual. The Bible promises faithful people that God watches over them constantly. The Bible promises people who lack faith that they may *have* faith if they desire it. In short, there is no human difficulty that is excluded from the promises of the Bible.

The book you are holding is a comprehensive attempt to gather together the Bible's promises on every possible topic of concern. The chapters are titled according to their topics ("Anger," "Heaven," "Marriage," "Money," etc.) and arranged alphabetically.

We hope this book will lead you to a richer understanding and appreciation for the God who keeps his promises.

Contents

Adultery	1
Aging	4
Alcohol and Other Substance Abuse	6
Angels	9
Anger	12
Baptism of the Spirit/Gifts of the Spirit	15
Children	19
Citizenship	22
Comfort in Times of Trouble	25
Confessing Sin	29
Conflict	31
Contentment	33
Death	35
The Devil	39
Discipline and Correction	42
Enemies	45
Eternal Life	47
Faith	50
Fear	53
Fellowship with God	56
Forgiving Others	58
Friends	60
God's Love for Us	63
God's Mercy	66
Guilt	68
Hate	70
Heaven	72
Hell	75
The Holy Spirit	77

Hope	81
Hypocrisy	84
Jesus' Second Coming	87
Joy	90
Judging Others	93
Loneliness	95
Loving God	96
Loving Others	98
Lying	101
Marriage	103
Mercy	106
Money	109
New Birth/New Life	113
Parents	116
Patience	119
Peace	122
Prayer	126
Pride and Conceit	130
Repentance	133
Revenge	136
Salvation	138
Self-Control and Self-Denial	142
Sexuality	145
Sickness	148
Sin and Redemption	152
Success	155
Temptation	158
The Tongue	161
Trusting God	164
Witnessing	166
Work	169
Worry and Anxiety	171

Adultery

One book about extramarital affairs is titled *The Myth of the Greener Grass*. For many people, even for many Christians, the grass always seems greener somewhere away from one's own spouse. The world used to take adultery seriously, but how things have changed! The tabloids and TV talk shows send the message that adultery is—well, normal. "Everybody's doing it" becomes a moral guideline, pushing aside that rather blunt statement in the Ten Commandments:

> *Do not commit adultery.*
>
> EXODUS 20:14

But the attractions of the "greener grass" are strong. God's Word takes a painfully realistic view of the lure of adultery—and of its consequences.

> *The lips of an immoral woman are as sweet as honey, and her mouth is smoother than oil. But the result is as bitter as poison, sharp as a double-edged sword.*
>
> PROVERBS 5:3-4

> *A prostitute will bring you to poverty, and sleeping with another man's wife may cost you your very life. Can a man scoop fire into his lap and not be burned? Can he walk on hot coals and not blister his feet? So it is with the man who sleeps with another man's wife. He who embraces her will not go unpunished.*
>
> *The man who commits adultery is an utter fool, for he destroys his own soul.*
>
> PROVERBS 6:26-29, 32

Why be captivated, my son, with an immoral woman, or embrace the breasts of an adulterous woman?

For the LORD sees clearly what a man does, examining every path he takes. An evil man is held captive by his own sins; they are ropes that catch and hold him. He will die for lack of self-control; he will be lost because of his incredible folly.

PROVERBS 5:20-23

Give honor to marriage, and remain faithful to one another in marriage. God will surely judge people who are immoral and those who commit adultery.

HEBREWS 13:4

We don't like to think of God as a judge, do we? It goes against the modern grain, for we are expected to be tolerant and nonjudgmental. But the Bible pulls no punches: God is a merciful Father—and also the great Judge. The prohibition of adultery isn't just some arbitrary rule designed to kill our pleasure. It's a moral guide to being the type of person God wants for his eternal Kingdom.

The apostle Paul, confronted with the many sexual sins of the church of Corinth, made this clear:

Run away from sexual sin! No other sin so clearly affects the body as this one does. For sexual immorality is a sin against your own body.

1 CORINTHIANS 6:18

Don't you know that those who do wrong will have no share in the Kingdom of God? Don't fool yourselves. Those who indulge in sexual sin, who are idol worshipers, adulterers, male prostitutes, homosexuals, thieves, greedy people, drunkards, abusers, and swindlers—none of these will have a share in the Kingdom of God.

1 CORINTHIANS 6:9-10

Harsh words, aren't they? Lumping adulterers together with thieves, swindlers, and drunkards. In spite of the world's indifference toward adultery, the Christian standard is higher. Jesus took the "no-adultery" standard one step further:

> You have heard that the law of Moses says, "Do not commit adultery." But I say, anyone who even looks at a woman with lust in his eye has already committed adultery with her in his heart.
>
> MATTHEW 5:27-28

Did Jesus mean that every wayward glance was as wicked as the act itself? More likely he was saying something we all know too well: Our heart and imagination can be sinful even when we're unwilling to commit the actual sin. There are many adulterers in the world. There are even more people who fantasize, who are unfaithful *inside* while remaining faithful *outside*. Jesus' message to people who want to be part of God's Kingdom was this: Keep your body *and* your mind from being unfaithful.

> From the heart come evil thoughts, murder, adultery, all other sexual immorality, theft, lying, and slander. These are what defile you.
>
> MATTHEW 15:19-20

See also Marriage, Sexuality, Temptation.

Aging

Who wants to grow old? Comedian George Burns, who lived past one hundred, quipped, "It's better than the alternative." But is it? For the Christian, the alternative to living on in this world is—heaven. God's Word has a lot to say about heaven, but it also has a lot to say about aging. We can be thankful that the Lord has a more gracious attitude toward aging than our youth-obsessed society does.

> *Gray hair is a crown of glory; it is gained by living a godly life.*
> PROVERBS 16:31

> *The glory of the young is their strength; the gray hair of experience is the splendor of the old.*
> PROVERBS 20:29

What an unfashionable idea! Gray hair as a "crown of glory," a sign of "experience." The Almighty's values are a far cry from our own. Instead of being disposable seniors, the elderly are promised God's continuing concern.

> *I will be your God throughout your lifetime—until your hair is white with age. I made you, and I will care for you. I will carry you along and save you.*
> ISAIAH 46:4

> *Grandchildren are the crowning glory of the aged.*
> PROVERBS 17:6

Show your fear of God by standing up in the presence of elderly people and showing respect for the aged. I am the LORD.

LEVITICUS 19:32

The godly will flourish like palm trees and grow strong like the cedars of Lebanon. For they are transplanted into the LORD's own house. They flourish in the courts of our God. Even in old age they will still produce fruit; they will remain vital and green.

PSALM 92:12-14

Alcohol and Other
Substance Abuse

In recent years people have become more conscious of the abuse of alcohol and other substances. But in spite of our growing awareness of the personal and social harm that is done, we seem to be losing the drug war, and alcoholism is on the rise.

What does the Bible say about such practices? Well, you will search in vain for a verse that says, "Don't drink alcohol, period." And the Bible says nothing whatsoever about illegal drugs, since they weren't available in Bible times. But the Bible does have much to say about any substance that harms us mentally or spiritually. Happily, it also has much to say about the alternatives to a chemical high.

> *Wine produces mockers; liquor leads to brawls. Whoever is led astray by drink cannot be wise.* .
>
> PROVERBS 20:1

> *Those who love pleasure become poor; wine and luxury are not the way to riches.*
>
> PROVERBS 21:17

> *Do not carouse with drunkards and gluttons, for they are on their way to poverty. Too much sleep clothes a person with rags.*
> *Who has anguish? Who has sorrow? Who is always fighting? Who is always complaining? Who has unnecessary bruises? Who has bloodshot eyes? It is the one who spends long hours in the taverns, trying out new drinks. Don't let the sparkle and smooth taste of wine deceive you. For in the end it*

bites like a poisonous serpent; it stings like a viper. You will see hallucinations, and you will say crazy things. You will stagger like a sailor tossed at sea, clinging to a swaying mast. And you will say, "They hit me, but I didn't feel it. I didn't even know it when they beat me up. When will I wake up so I can have another drink?"

PROVERBS 23:20-21, 29-35

Destruction is certain for you who get up early to begin long drinking bouts that last late into the night.

Destruction is certain for those who are heroes when it comes to drinking, who boast about all the liquor they can hold. They take bribes to pervert justice. They let the wicked go free while punishing the innocent.

Therefore, they will all disappear like burning straw. Their roots will rot and their flowers wither, for they have rejected the law of the LORD Almighty. They have despised the word of the Holy One of Israel.

ISAIAH 5:11, 22-24

Watch out! Don't let me find you living in careless ease and drunkenness, and filled with the worries of this life. Don't let that day catch you unaware, as in a trap. For that day will come upon everyone living on the earth.

LUKE 21:34-35

Those who belong to the Kingdom of God should lead lives that reflect what God desires for his people. Paul makes it clear that this does not include altering our mind and behavior with chemical substances instead of finding our fulfillment in God.

We should be decent and true in everything we do, so that everyone can approve of our behavior. Don't participate in wild parties and getting drunk, or in adultery and immoral living, or in fighting and jealousy.

ROMANS 13:13

Don't be drunk with wine, because that will ruin your life. Instead, let the Holy Spirit fill and control you.

EPHESIANS 5:18

See also Sickness, Temptation.

Angels

Angels are God's messengers, invisible except when they assume a shape to appear before human beings. We don't know what they look like, except that they appear as grand, awe-inspiring beings—not the chubby, sweet-faced infants in old artworks. People in the Bible—and Christians of later times—usually speak of angels as magnificent beings who inspire awe but also give comfort.

Angels appear in many places in the Bible, but the most familiar passages remind us of their role as protectors and comforters of God's people.

> *The angel of the LORD guards all who fear him, and he rescues them.*
>
> PSALM 34:7

> *If you make the LORD your refuge, if you make the Most High your shelter, no evil will conquer you; no plague will come near your dwelling. For he orders his angels to protect you wherever you go. They will hold you with their hands to keep you from striking your foot on a stone.*
>
> PSALM 91:9-12

> *The high priest and his friends, who were Sadducees, reacted with violent jealousy. They arrested the apostles and put them in the jail. But an angel of the Lord came at night, opened the gates of the jail, and brought them out.*
>
> ACTS 5:17-19

> *The night before Peter was to be placed on trial, he was asleep, chained between two soldiers, with others standing*

9

*guard at the prison gate. Suddenly, there was a bright light in
the cell, and an angel of the Lord stood before Peter. The
angel tapped him on the side to awaken him and said,
"Quick! Get up!" And the chains fell off his wrists. Then
the angel told him, "Get dressed and put on your sandals."
And he did. "Now put on your coat and follow me," the
angel ordered.*

*So Peter left the cell, following the angel. But all the time he
thought it was a vision. He didn't realize it was really happening. They passed the first and second guard posts and came to
the iron gate to the street, and this opened to them all by itself.
So they passed through and started walking down the street,
and then the angel suddenly left him.*

*Peter finally realized what had happened. "It's really true!"
he said to himself. "The Lord has sent his angel and saved me
from Herod and from what the Jews were hoping to do to
me!"*

ACTS 12:6-11

*Beware that you don't despise a single one of these little
ones. For I tell you that in heaven their angels are always in
the presence of my heavenly Father.*

MATTHEW 18:10

*I assure you of this: If anyone acknowledges me publicly here
on earth, I, the Son of Man, will openly acknowledge that
person in the presence of God's angels. But if anyone denies
me here on earth, I will deny that person before God's
angels.*

LUKE 12:8-9

*There is joy in the presence of God's angels when even one
sinner repents.*

LUKE 15:10

Jesus and the apostle Paul promised that angels would play a key role in the second coming of Christ. The angels are "reapers," gathering in the harvest of God's faithful people. They are also "heralds," announcing Jesus' glorious arrival on earth.

> I, the Son of Man, will send my angels, and they will remove from my Kingdom everything that causes sin and all who do evil, and they will throw them into the furnace and burn them. There will be weeping and gnashing of teeth. Then the godly will shine like the sun in their Father's Kingdom. Anyone who is willing to hear should listen and understand!
>
> MATTHEW 13:41-43

> Then at last, the sign of the coming of the Son of Man will appear in the heavens, and there will be deep mourning among all the nations of the earth. And they will see the Son of Man arrive on the clouds of heaven with power and great glory. And he will send forth his angels with the sound of a mighty trumpet blast, and they will gather together his chosen ones from the farthest ends of the earth and heaven.
>
> MATTHEW 24:30-31

> The Lord himself will come down from heaven with a commanding shout, with the call of the archangel, and with the trumpet call of God. First, all the Christians who have died will rise from their graves. Then, together with them, we who are still alive and remain on the earth will be caught up in the clouds to meet the Lord in the air and remain with him forever. So comfort and encourage each other with these words.
>
> 1 THESSALONIANS 4:16-18

See also The Devil.

Anger

The Bible doesn't say to never be angry. In fact, it tells how Jesus, the perfect man, the Son of God, drove the greedy money-changers out of the Temple (John 2:14-15). We are expected to be angry at oppression, at the injustice in the world, at blatant cruelty—in other words, at *sin*.

But this isn't the kind of anger most of us feel. Don't we usually feel anger—sometimes boiling rage—at being slighted, ignored, insulted? Don't pride and ego lead to most of our anger? This kind of anger the Bible warns against. It promises sad consequences if we persist in it.

> My dear brothers and sisters, be quick to listen, slow to speak, and slow to get angry. Your anger can never make things right in God's sight.
>
> JAMES 1:19-20

> Don't be quick-tempered, for anger is the friend of fools.
>
> ECCLESIASTES 7:9

> Dear friends, never avenge yourselves. Leave that to God. For it is written, "I will take vengeance; I will repay those who deserve it," says the Lord. Instead, do what the Scriptures say: "If your enemies are hungry, feed them. If they are thirsty, give them something to drink, and they will be ashamed of what they have done to you." Don't let evil get the best of you, but conquer evil by doing good.
>
> ROMANS 12:19-21

A gentle answer turns away wrath, but harsh words stir up anger.

PROVERBS 15:1

Stop your anger! Turn from your rage! Do not envy others—it only leads to harm.

PSALM 37:8

A fool is quick-tempered, but a wise person stays calm when insulted.

PROVERBS 12:16

Stay away from fools, for you won't find knowledge there.

PROVERBS 14:7

Keep away from angry, short-tempered people, or you will learn to be like them and endanger your soul.

PROVERBS 22:24-25

Mockers can get a whole town agitated, but those who are wise will calm anger.

PROVERBS 29:8

A hot-tempered person starts fights and gets into all kinds of sin.

PROVERBS 29:22

I say, if you are angry with someone, you are subject to judgment! If you call someone an idiot, you are in danger of being brought before the high council. And if you curse someone, you are in danger of the fires of hell.

MATTHEW 5:22

"Don't sin by letting anger gain control over you." Don't let the sun go down while you are still angry.

EPHESIANS 4:26

Now is the time to get rid of anger, rage, malicious behavior, slander, and dirty language. Don't lie to each other, for you have stripped off your old evil nature and all its wicked deeds. In its place you have clothed yourselves with a brand-new nature that is continually being renewed as you learn more and more about Christ, who created this new nature within you.

COLOSSIANS 3:8-10

See also Hate, Pride and Conceit, Self-Control and Self-Denial.

Baptism of the Spirit/Gifts of the Spirit

Baptism is done with water, but the Bible talks about another baptism that is much more important than the water ritual. This is the baptism of the Spirit, a teaching that was neglected for many years but has been given a renewed emphasis in many churches. This renewed interest in the Spirit's work is something to rejoice over. Christians of past times knew that without the Spirit there is only the lifeless, mechanical performance of religious duties.

> *After I have poured out my rains again, I will pour out my Spirit upon all people. Your sons and daughters will prophesy. Your old men will dream dreams. Your young men will see visions. In those days, I will pour out my Spirit even on servants, men and women alike.*
>
> JOEL 2:28-29

> *[John the Baptist:] "I baptize with water those who turn from their sins and turn to God. But someone is coming soon who is far greater than I am—so much greater that I am not even worthy to be his slave. He will baptize you with the Holy Spirit and with fire."*
>
> MATTHEW 3:11

> *Jesus replied, "The truth is, no one can enter the Kingdom of God without being born of water and the Spirit."*
>
> JOHN 3:5

*Some of us are Jews, some are Gentiles, some are slaves,
and some are free. But we have all been baptized into
Christ's body by one Spirit, and we have all received the
same Spirit.*

1 CORINTHIANS 12:13

*He washed away our sins and gave us a new life through the
Holy Spirit.*

TITUS 3:5

You cannot talk about the Spirit without speaking of spiritual gifts. While the Spirit himself is *the* gift to Christians, the Bible also promises that each of us is given a special gift through the Spirit.

*God verified the message by signs and wonders and various
miracles and by giving gifts of the Holy Spirit whenever he
chose to do so.*

HEBREWS 2:4

*There are different kinds of spiritual gifts, but it is the same
Holy Spirit who is the source of them all. There are different
kinds of service in the church, but it is the same Lord we are
serving. There are different ways God works in our lives,
but it is the same God who does the work through all of us.
God manifests the Spirit through each person for the good of
the entire church.*

*To one person the Spirit gives a word of special wisdom; to
another he gives the gift of special knowledge. The Spirit gives
special faith to another, and to someone else he gives the power
to heal the sick. He gives one person the power to perform
miracles, and to another the ability to prophesy. He gives
someone else the ability to distinguish between spirits. Still
another person is given the ability to speak in different kinds of
tongues, and another is given the ability to interpret what is
being said. It is the same and only Holy Spirit who distributes*

these gifts. He alone decides which gift each person should have.

The human body has many parts, but the many parts make up only one body. So it is with the body of Christ. Some of us are Jews, some are Gentiles, some are slaves, and some are free. But we have all been baptized into Christ's body by one Spirit, and we have all received the same Spirit.

Yes, the body has many different parts, not just one part. If the foot says, "I am not a part of the body because I am not a hand," that does not make it any less a part of the body. And if the ear says, "I am not part of the body because I am only an ear and not an eye," would that make it any less a part of the body? Suppose the whole body were an eye—then how would you hear? Or if your whole body were just one big ear, how could you smell anything?

But God made our bodies with many parts, and he has put each part just where he wants it. What a strange thing a body would be if it had only one part! Yes, there are many parts, but only one body. The eye can never say to the hand, "I don't need you." The head can't say to the feet, "I don't need you."

In fact, some of the parts that seem weakest and least important are really the most necessary. And the parts we regard as less honorable are those we clothe with the greatest care. So we carefully protect from the eyes of others those parts that should not be seen, while other parts do not require this special care. So God has put the body together in such a way that extra honor and care are given to those parts that have less dignity. This makes for harmony among the members, so that all the members care for each other equally. If one part suffers, all the parts suffer with it, and if one part is honored, all the parts are glad.

Now all of you together are Christ's body, and each one of you is a separate and necessary part of it. Here is a list of some of the members that God has placed in the body of Christ: first are apostles, second are prophets, third are teachers, then those who do miracles, those who have the gift of healing, those who can help others, those who can get others to work together, those who speak in different kinds of tongues. Is everyone an apostle? Of course not. Is everyone a prophet? No. Are all teachers? Does everyone have the power to do miracles? Does everyone have the gift of healing? Of course not. Does God give all of us the ability to speak in tongues? Can everyone interpret tongues? No! And in any event, you should desire the most helpful gifts.

1 CORINTHIANS 12:4-31

See also The Holy Spirit.

Children

You will find many promises in the Bible concerning children. Some promises are negative: children who go astray can be a terrible burden to bear. But other promises are positive: children themselves are a blessing, especially if reared with discipline and kindness. Hymn writer John Bowring claimed that "a happy family is an earlier heaven."

Whether the family turns out good or bad is, of course, partly the parents' own responsibility.

> Children are a gift from the LORD; they are a reward from him. Children born to a young man are like sharp arrows in a warrior's hands. How happy is the man whose quiver is full of them! He will not be put to shame when he confronts his accusers at the city gates.
>
> PSALM 127:3-5

> Grandchildren are the crowning glory of the aged; parents are the pride of their children.
>
> PROVERBS 17:6

What happens to weak-willed parents who can't—or won't—insist on discipline in the home? The Bible gives a painfully realistic answer to that:

> If you refuse to discipline your children, it proves you don't love them; if you love your children, you will be prompt to discipline them.
>
> PROVERBS 13:24

Discipline your children while there is hope. If you don't, you will ruin their lives.

PROVERBS 19:18

To discipline and reprimand a child produces wisdom, but a mother is disgraced by an undisciplined child.

PROVERBS 29:15

Teach your children to choose the right path, and when they are older, they will remain upon it.

PROVERBS 22:6

Don't fail to correct your children. They won't die if you spank them. Physical discipline may well save them from death.

PROVERBS 23:13-14

Discipline is not the whole duty of parents. If they are believers, they also have a duty to pass on their own beliefs to their children.

You must commit yourselves wholeheartedly to these commands I am giving you today. Repeat them again and again to your children. Talk about them when you are at home and when you are away on a journey, when you are lying down and when you are getting up again. Tie them to your hands as a reminder, and wear them on your forehead. Write them on the doorposts of your house and on your gates.

DEUTERONOMY 6:6-9

Not all the Bible's promises are to parents. Children, too, have some words addressed to them from the Lord. Just as the Bible promises good to people who are thankful toward God, it promises blessing to those who are grateful to their parents.

My son, obey your father's commands, and don't neglect your mother's teaching. Keep their words always in your heart. Tie them around your neck. Wherever you walk, their counsel can lead you. When you sleep, they will protect you. When you wake up in the morning, they will advise you. For these commands and this teaching are a lamp to light the way ahead of you. The correction of discipline is the way to life.

PROVERBS 6:20-23

Listen to your father, who gave you life, and don't despise your mother's experience when she is old.

PROVERBS 23:22

A wise child accepts a parent's discipline; a young mocker refuses to listen.

PROVERBS 13:1

Only a fool despises a parent's discipline; whoever learns from correction is wise.

PROVERBS 15:5

Even children are known by the way they act, whether their conduct is pure and right.

PROVERBS 20:11

The father of godly children has cause for joy. What a pleasure it is to have wise children. So give your parents joy! May she who gave you birth be happy. O my son, give me your heart. May your eyes delight in my ways of wisdom.

PROVERBS 23:24-26

See also Marriage, Parents.

Citizenship

The Bible shows no reason people of faith cannot also be a good citizen. In fact, they are encouraged to be both. But, as Jesus predicted, he and his followers would suffer hardship, some of it at the hands of government officials. The New Testament never shows a Christian showing disrespect or violence toward these people. Still, there is a tension in the Christian life: our first loyalty is to God, not to the state. God promises us inner peace—not necessarily peaceful coexistence with a government that may detest and even persecute us.

> The captain went with his Temple guards and arrested them [the apostles], but without violence, for they were afraid the people would kill them if they treated the apostles roughly. Then they brought the apostles in before the council. "Didn't we tell you never again to teach in this man's name?" the high priest demanded. "Instead, you have filled all Jerusalem with your teaching about Jesus, and you intend to blame us for his death!"
>
> But Peter and the apostles replied, "We must obey God rather than human authority."
>
> ACTS 5:26-29

> The Pharisees met together to think of a way to trap Jesus into saying something for which they could accuse him. They decided to send some of their disciples, along with the supporters of Herod, to ask him this question: "Teacher, we know how honest you are. You teach about the way of God regardless of the consequences. You are impartial and don't

play favorites. Now tell us what you think about this: Is it right to pay taxes to the Roman government or not?"

But Jesus knew their evil motives. "You hypocrites!" he said. "Whom are you trying to fool with your trick questions? Here, show me the Roman coin used for the tax." When they handed him the coin, he asked, "Whose picture and title are stamped on it?"

"Caesar's," they replied.

"Well, then," he said, "give to Caesar what belongs to him. But everything that belongs to God must be given to God."

MATTHEW 22:15-21

After Jesus' arrest he faced Pilate, the Roman governor. Pilate assumed he had a political agitator on his hands, but Jesus assured him that the revolution he was staging was in human hearts, not in the area of politics.

Pilate went back inside and called for Jesus to be brought to him. "Are you the King of the Jews?" he asked him.

Jesus replied, "Is this your own question, or did others tell you about me?"

"Am I a Jew?" Pilate asked. "Your own people and their leading priests brought you here. Why? What have you done?"

Then Jesus answered, "I am not an earthly king. If I were, my followers would have fought when I was arrested by the Jewish leaders. But my Kingdom is not of this world."

Pilate replied, "You are a king then?"

"You say that I am a king, and you are right," Jesus said. "I was born for that purpose. And I came to bring truth to the world. All who love the truth recognize that what I say is true."

JOHN 18:33-37

Obey the government, for God is the one who put it there. All governments have been placed in power by God. So *those who refuse to obey the laws of the land are refusing to obey God, and punishment will follow. For the authorities do not frighten people who are doing right, but they frighten those who do wrong. So do what they say, and you will get along well. The authorities are sent by God to help you. But if you are doing something wrong, of course you should be afraid, for you will be punished. The authorities are established by God for that very purpose, to punish those who do wrong. So you must obey the government for two reasons: to keep from being punished and to keep a clear conscience.*

Pay your taxes, too, for these same reasons. For government workers need to be paid so they can keep on doing the work God intended them to do. Give to everyone what you owe them: Pay your taxes and import duties, and give respect and honor to all to whom it is due.

ROMANS 13:1-7

Comfort in Times of Trouble

What does God promise his people? Relief from all troubles in the next world, relief from *some* troubles in this life. Faithful people throughout the centuries have been witnesses to dramatic deliverances from sickness, from financial woes, from all manner of troubles. Flesh-and-blood human beings have testified to miracles. They do happen.

But not always. Sometimes we aren't relieved by God. Sometimes we merely *endure*. This isn't such a bad thing. We are never nearer to God than when we are troubled. In times of comfort and ease, we might forget him. But in the worst of times, we suddenly remember, *Ah, what if I asked God for help?* Sometimes the answer is the help we pray for. Sometimes the answer is "Lean on me, and you will survive and thrive."

> *Whom have I in heaven but you? I desire you more than anything on earth. My health may fail, and my spirit may grow weak, but God remains the strength of my heart; he is mine forever.*
>
> PSALM 73:25-26
>
> *Remember your promise to me, for it is my only hope. Your promise revives me; it comforts me in all my troubles.*
>
> PSALM 119:49-50
>
> *The LORD is my shepherd; I have everything I need. He lets me rest in green meadows; he leads me beside peaceful streams. He renews my strength. He guides me along right paths, bringing honor to his name.*

Even when I walk through the dark valley of death, I will not be afraid, for you are close beside me. Your rod and your staff protect and comfort me.

PSALM 23:1-4

The LORD is my rock, my fortress, and my savior; my God is my rock, in whom I find protection. He is my shield, the strength of my salvation, and my stronghold.

PSALM 18:2

Weeping may go on all night, but joy comes with the morning.

PSALM 30:5

God is our refuge and strength, always ready to help in times of trouble. So we will not fear, even if earthquakes come and the mountains crumble into the sea.

PSALM 46:1-2

You have allowed me to suffer much hardship, but you will restore me to life again and lift me up from the depths of the earth.

PSALM 71:20

The LORD is like a father to his children, tender and compassionate to those who fear him.

PSALM 103:13

Those who plant in tears will harvest with shouts of joy. They weep as they go to plant their seed, but they sing as they return with the harvest.

PSALM 126:5-6

He heals the brokenhearted, binding up their wounds.

PSALM 147:3

Don't be afraid, for I am with you. Do not be dismayed, for I am your God. I will strengthen you. I will help you. I will uphold you with my victorious right hand.

ISAIAH 41:10

When you go through deep waters and great trouble, I will be with you. When you go through rivers of difficulty, you will not drown! When you walk through the fire of oppression, you will not be burned up; the flames will not consume you.

ISAIAH 43:2

God blesses those who mourn, for they will be comforted.

God blesses those who are persecuted because they live for God, for the Kingdom of Heaven is theirs.

God blesses you when you are mocked and persecuted and lied about because you are my followers. Be happy about it! Be very glad! For a great reward awaits you in heaven. And remember, the ancient prophets were persecuted, too.

MATTHEW 5:4, 10-12

Not even a sparrow, worth only half a penny, can fall to the ground without your Father knowing it. And the very hairs on your head are all numbered. So don't be afraid; you are more valuable to him than a whole flock of sparrows.

MATTHEW 10:29-31

Jesus said, "Come to me, all of you who are weary and carry heavy burdens, and I will give you rest. Take my yoke upon you. Let me teach you, because I am humble and gentle, and you will find rest for your souls. For my yoke fits perfectly, and the burden I give you is light."

MATTHEW 11:28-30

We are pressed on every side by troubles, but we are not crushed and broken. We are perplexed, but we don't give up and quit.

That is why we never give up. Though our bodies are dying, our spirits are being renewed every day. For our present troubles are quite small and won't last very long. Yet they produce for us an immeasurably great glory that will last forever!

2 CORINTHIANS 4:8, 16-17

See also Patience, Peace, Sickness, Worry and Anxiety.

Confessing Sin

"Confession is good for the soul"—so says the old cliché. Like many clichés, it has the virtue of being true.

For the Christian, confession is not an option. We sin, and we confess, and our life with God goes on. It can't be otherwise. Augustine, the great Christian teacher in the Roman Empire, noted that "the confession of evil works is the first beginning of good works."

> *People who cover over their sins will not prosper. But if they confess and forsake them, they will receive mercy.*
>
> PROVERBS 28:13

> *Oh, what joy for those whose rebellion is forgiven, whose sin is put out of sight! Yes, what joy for those whose record the LORD has cleared of sin, whose lives are lived in complete honesty!*
>
> *When I refused to confess my sin, I was weak and miserable, and I groaned all day long. Day and night your hand of discipline was heavy on me. My strength evaporated like water in the summer heat.*
>
> *Finally, I confessed all my sins to you and stopped trying to hide them. I said to myself, "I will confess my rebellion to the LORD." And you forgave me! All my guilt is gone.*
>
> *Therefore, let all the godly confess their rebellion to you while there is time, that they may not drown in the floodwaters of judgment.*
>
> PSALM 32:1-6

The great "sin song" of the Bible, Psalm 51, was supposedly written by King David when he felt guilt over his adultery. The most beautiful thing about this psalm is David's full confidence that God will accept his repentant heart and restore his spiritual health.

> *Have mercy on me, O God, because of your unfailing love. Because of your great compassion, blot out the stain of my sins. Wash me clean from my guilt. Purify me from my sin.*
>
> *For I recognize my shameful deeds—they haunt me day and night. Against you, and you alone, have I sinned; I have done what is evil in your sight. You will be proved right in what you say, and your judgment against me is just.*
>
> *For I was born a sinner—yes, from the moment my mother conceived me. But you desire honesty from the heart, so you can teach me to be wise in my inmost being.*
>
> *Purify me from my sins, and I will be clean; wash me, and I will be whiter than snow. Oh, give me back my joy again; you have broken me—now let me rejoice. Don't keep looking at my sins. Remove the stain of my guilt. Create in me a clean heart, O God. Renew a right spirit within me.*
>
> PSALM 51:1-10

> *"As surely as I live," says the Lord, "every knee will bow to me and every tongue will confess allegiance to God." Yes, each of us will have to give a personal account to God.*
>
> ROMANS 14:11-12

> *If we confess our sins to him, he is faithful and just to forgive us and to cleanse us from every wrong.*
>
> 1 JOHN 1:9

> *Confess your sins to each other and pray for each other so that you may be healed. The earnest prayer of a righteous person has great power and wonderful results.*
>
> JAMES 5:16

See also Guilt, Repentance, Sin and Redemption.

Conflict

Wherever there are two human beings, there is the potential for fighting. Part of the human condition is that people do quarrel. And some of the bitterest fights are between people who are closest: husband and wife, parent and child, siblings, longtime friends—even fellow Christians.

The Bible has a lot to say about the source of conflicts and how to squelch them.

Hatred stirs up quarrels, but love covers all offenses.

PROVERBS 10:12

Pride leads to arguments; those who take advice are wise.

PROVERBS 13:10

A gentle answer turns away wrath, but harsh words stir up anger.

PROVERBS 15:1

Anyone who loves to quarrel loves sin; anyone who speaks boastfully invites disaster.

PROVERBS 17:19

Avoiding a fight is a mark of honor; only fools insist on quarreling.

PROVERBS 20:3

A hot-tempered person starts fights and gets into all kinds of sin.

PROVERBS 29:22

You are still controlled by your own sinful desires. You are jealous of one another and quarrel with each other. Doesn't that prove you are controlled by your own desires? You are acting like people who don't belong to the Lord.

1 CORINTHIANS 3:3

See also Hate, Peace.

Contentment

The comic Will Rogers described advertising as "making people want what they don't need and pay for it with money they don't have." He understood a basic principle of advertising: make people discontent—make them feel their lives would be better if they had product X. "My life would be fine if only I had . . ." What? A better job? A new car? More vacation time? Bigger muscles? A new hair color?

In fact, this feeling didn't begin with the age of advertising. It's as old as humanity. The Bible writers were familiar with it. They were also familiar with an ageless truth: nothing brings contentment except living within God's will.

A relaxed attitude lengthens life; jealousy rots it away.
PROVERBS 14:30

For the happy heart, life is a continual feast.
PROVERBS 15:15

It is better to be poor and godly than rich and dishonest.
PROVERBS 16:8

A dry crust eaten in peace is better than a great feast with strife.

PROVERBS 17:1

A cheerful heart is good medicine, but a broken spirit saps a person's strength.

PROVERBS 17:22

Don't envy sinners, but always continue to fear the LORD.

PROVERBS 23:17

Enjoy what you have rather than desiring what you don't have. Just dreaming about nice things is meaningless; it is like chasing the wind.

ECCLESIASTES 6:9

Stay away from the love of money; be satisfied with what you have. For God has said, "I will never fail you. I will never forsake you."

HEBREWS 13:5

I have learned how to get along happily whether I have much or little. I know how to live on almost nothing or with everything. I have learned the secret of living in every situation, whether it is with a full stomach or empty, with plenty or little. For I can do everything with the help of Christ who gives me the strength I need.

PHILIPPIANS 4:11-13

True religion with contentment is great wealth. After all, we didn't bring anything with us when we came into the world, and we certainly cannot carry anything with us when we die. So if we have enough food and clothing, let us be content.

1 TIMOTHY 6:6-8

See also Peace, Success, Worry and Anxiety.

Death

Most of us fear death, don't we? We may *say* we believe in eternal life, in a heaven that is a life of bliss, a life much better than this world. But we *act* as if we fear death, and our actions speak louder than our words. We don't act much different from people who claim to have no belief at all in heaven and hell. Isn't it amazing that centuries ago, Christians sometimes celebrated a believer's funeral as his or her "birthday," the day of the person's entry into heaven? They celebrated because they really believed it was so.

We need to go back to the Bible. It reminds us many times that nothing, not even death, can snatch God's people from him.

> *Even when I walk through the dark valley of death, I will not be afraid, for you are close beside me.*
>
> PSALM 23:4

> *As for me, God will redeem my life. He will snatch me from the power of death.*
>
> PSALM 49:15

> *He will swallow up death forever! The Sovereign LORD will wipe away all tears.*
>
> ISAIAH 25:8

> *God blesses those who mourn, for they will be comforted.*
>
> MATTHEW 5:4

As to whether there will be a resurrection of the dead—haven't you ever read about this in the Scriptures? Long after Abraham, Isaac, and Jacob had died, God said, "I am the God of Abraham, the God of Isaac, and the God of Jacob." So he is the God of the living, not the dead.

MATTHEW 22:31-32

Humans can reproduce only human life, but the Holy Spirit gives new life from heaven.

JOHN 3:6

All who believe in God's Son have eternal life. Those who don't obey the Son will never experience eternal life, but the wrath of God remains upon them.

JOHN 3:36

I assure you, those who listen to my message and believe in God who sent me have eternal life. They will never be condemned for their sins, but they have already passed from death into life.

JOHN 5:24

Can anything ever separate us from Christ's love? Does it mean he no longer loves us if we have trouble or calamity, or are persecuted, or are hungry or cold or in danger or threatened with death? . . . No, despite all these things, overwhelming victory is ours through Christ, who loved us.

And I am convinced that nothing can ever separate us from his love. Death can't, and life can't. The angels can't, and the demons can't. Our fears for today, our worries about tomorrow, and even the powers of hell can't keep God's love away.

ROMANS 8:35-38

Let me tell you a wonderful secret God has revealed to us. Not all of us will die, but we will all be transformed. It will happen in a moment, in the blinking of an eye, when the last trumpet is blown. For when the trumpet sounds, the Christians who have died will be raised with transformed bodies. And then we who are living will be transformed so that we will never die. For our perishable earthly bodies must be transformed into heavenly bodies that will never die.

When this happens—when our perishable earthly bodies have been transformed into heavenly bodies that will never die—then at last the Scriptures will come true: "Death is swallowed up in victory. O death, where is your victory? O death, where is your sting?"

1 CORINTHIANS 15:51-55

To me, living is for Christ, and dying is even better. Yet if I live, that means fruitful service for Christ. I really don't know which is better. I'm torn between two desires: Sometimes I want to live, and sometimes I long to go and be with Christ.

PHILIPPIANS 1:21-23

Because God's children are human beings—made of flesh and blood—Jesus also became flesh and blood by being born in human form. For only as a human being could he die, and only by dying could he break the power of the Devil, who had the power of death. Only in this way could he deliver those who have lived all their lives as slaves to the fear of dying.

HEBREWS 2:14-15

I saw a great white throne, and I saw the one who was sitting on it. . . . I saw the dead, both great and small, standing before God's throne. And the books were opened, including the Book of Life. And the dead were judged according to the things written in the books, according to what they had done. The sea gave up the dead in it, and death and the grave gave up the dead in them. They were all judged according to their deeds. And death and the grave were thrown into the lake of fire. This is the second death—the lake of fire. And anyone whose name was not found recorded in the Book of Life was thrown into the lake of fire.

REVELATION 20:11-15

See also Eternal Life, Heaven, Hell, Hope, Jesus' Second Coming.

The Devil

Can people in our day and age really believe in Satan, an actual *Devil*? Why not? With so many people believing in reincarnation, astral projection, and other New Age beliefs, why not a Devil? Unlike those other beliefs, belief in Satan is clearly taught in the Bible and has been an article of faith for Christians for two thousand years.

Maybe we've outgrown the old pictures of the Devil, with horns, a pitchfork, and a pointy tail. Fine. The Bible shows no concern about the Devil's looks. The Bible *is* concerned with a spiritual being that acts in direct opposition to a loving, merciful God who wants people to lead full, rewarding lives.

> *If I am casting out demons by the Spirit of God, then the Kingdom of God has arrived among you.*
>
> MATTHEW 12:28

> *When the seventy-two disciples returned, they joyfully reported to him, "Lord, even the demons obey us when we use your name!"*
>
> *"Yes," he told them, "I saw Satan falling from heaven as a flash of lightning! And I have given you authority over all the power of the enemy, and you can walk among snakes and scorpions and crush them. Nothing will injure you. But don't rejoice just because evil spirits obey you; rejoice because your names are registered as citizens of heaven."*
>
> LUKE 10:17-20

> *You know what happened all through Judea, beginning in Galilee after John the Baptist began preaching. And no*

doubt you know that God anointed Jesus of Nazareth with the Holy Spirit and with power. Then Jesus went around doing good and healing all who were oppressed by the Devil, for God was with him.

ACTS 10:37-38

When Jesus appeared to Paul on the Damascus road, he specifically mentioned tearing down the works of the Devil.

I am going to send you to the Gentiles, to open their eyes so they may turn from darkness to light, and from the power of Satan to God. Then they will receive forgiveness for their sins and be given a place among God's people, who are set apart by faith in me.

ACTS 26:17-18

The apostle Paul, like Jesus, understood the incredible power of Satan. He understood even better that God was much stronger and would ultimately triumph.

The Bible's classic passage about our safety from Satan is found in Paul's letter to the Ephesians. It reminds us that, frail though we are, we have a divine "armor" to protect us against the powers of darkness.

Put on all of God's armor so that you will be able to stand firm against all strategies and tricks of the Devil. For we are not fighting against people made of flesh and blood, but against the evil rulers and authorities of the unseen world, against those mighty powers of darkness who rule this world, and against wicked spirits in the heavenly realms.

Use every piece of God's armor to resist the enemy in the time of evil, so that after the battle you will still be standing firm. Stand your ground, putting on the sturdy belt of truth and the body armor of God's righteousness. For shoes, put on the peace that comes from the Good News, so that you will be fully prepared. In every battle you will need faith as your shield to stop the fiery arrows aimed at you by Satan. Put on salvation as your helmet, and take the sword of the Spirit, which is the word of God.

EPHESIANS 6:11-17

Humble yourselves before God. Resist the Devil, and he will flee from you. Draw close to God, and God will draw close to you.

JAMES 4:7-8

Be careful! Watch out for attacks from the Devil, your great enemy. He prowls around like a roaring lion, looking for some victim to devour. Take a firm stand against him, and be strong in your faith. Remember that your Christian brothers and sisters all over the world are going through the same kind of suffering you are.

1 PETER 5:8-9

When people keep on sinning, it shows they belong to the Devil, who has been sinning since the beginning. But the Son of God came to destroy these works of the Devil. Those who have been born into God's family do not sin, because God's life is in them. So they can't keep on sinning, because they have been born of God. So now we can tell who are children of God and who are children of the Devil. Anyone who does not obey God's commands and does not love other Christians does not belong to God.

1 JOHN 3:8-10

See also Hell, Sin and Redemption, Temptation.

Discipline and Correction

Being nonjudgmental is considered a virtue these days. Odd, isn't it, since people hire golf pros and personal fitness trainers to critique and give advice? The golf pros know that the people they critique have the desire to improve their game, so people ask for their help. "Tell me what I'm doing wrong. I want to do better." We say this so easily to a sports trainer but don't like the idea of a "morality pro" disciplining us and correcting our mistakes. We even resist the idea of a God who acts in this way.

But that is exactly the kind of God revealed in the Bible. He wants us to do better, to improve, to show more love to him and to other people. God is one who loves, and genuine love involves discipline.

> *Just as a parent disciplines a child, the LORD your God disciplines you to help you.*
>
> *So obey the commands of the LORD your God by walking in his ways and fearing him.*
>
> DEUTERONOMY 8:5-6

> *Consider the joy of those corrected by God! Do not despise the chastening of the Almighty when you sin. For though he wounds, he also bandages. He strikes, but his hands also heal.*
>
> JOB 5:17-18

> *Fear of the LORD is the beginning of knowledge. Only fools despise wisdom and discipline.*
>
> PROVERBS 1:7

The LORD corrects those he loves, just as a father corrects a child in whom he delights.

PROVERBS 3:12

Don't bother rebuking mockers; they will only hate you. But the wise, when rebuked, will love you all the more.

PROVERBS 9:8

If you listen to constructive criticism, you will be at home among the wise.

If you reject criticism, you only harm yourself; but if you listen to correction, you grow in understanding.

PROVERBS 15:31-32

A single rebuke does more for a person of understanding than a hundred lashes on the back of a fool.

PROVERBS 17:10

Valid criticism is as treasured by the one who heeds it as jewelry made from finest gold.

PROVERBS 25:12

It is better to be criticized by a wise person than to be praised by a fool!

ECCLESIASTES 7:5

When we are judged and disciplined by the Lord, we will not be condemned with the world.

1 CORINTHIANS 11:32

Our present troubles are quite small and won't last very long. Yet they produce for us an immeasurably great glory that will last forever! So we don't look at the troubles we can see right now; rather, we look forward to what we have not yet seen. For the troubles we see will soon be over, but the joys to come will last forever.

2 CORINTHIANS 4:17-18

Have you entirely forgotten the encouraging words God spoke to you, his children? He said, "My child, don't ignore it when the Lord disciplines you, and don't be discouraged when he corrects you. For the Lord disciplines those he loves, and he punishes those he accepts as his children." As you endure this divine discipline, remember that God is treating you as his own children. Whoever heard of a child who was never disciplined? If God doesn't discipline you as he does all of his children, it means that you are illegitimate and are not really his children after all. Since we respect our earthly fathers who disciplined us, should we not all the more cheerfully submit to the discipline of our heavenly Father and live forever?

For our earthly fathers disciplined us for a few years, doing the best they knew how. But God's discipline is always right and good for us because it means we will share in his holiness. No discipline is enjoyable while it is happening—it is painful! But afterward there will be a quiet harvest of right living for those who are trained in this way.

HEBREWS 12:5-11

See also Patience.

Enemies

You won't find a promise in the Bible that you will never have enemies. In fact, the Bible makes it plain that people of faith will have enemies and will endure persecution.

But the Bible does promise us that God is greater than any enemy we will ever face. We may be small and weak compared with those who oppose us, but our enemies are small and weak compared with God. Even if justice is not done in this life, God guarantees that there is a final justice.

The LORD is for me, so I will not be afraid. What can mere mortals do to me? Yes, the LORD is for me; he will help me. I will look in triumph at those who hate me. It is better to trust the LORD than to put confidence in people. It is better to trust the LORD than to put confidence in princes.

PSALM 118:6-9

He will conceal me there when troubles come; he will hide me in his sanctuary. He will place me out of reach on a high rock. Then I will hold my head high, above my enemies who surround me.

PSALM 27:5-6

The LORD saves the godly; he is their fortress in times of trouble. The LORD helps them, rescuing them from the wicked. He saves them, and they find shelter in him.

PSALM 37:39-40

With God's help we will do mighty things, for he will trample down our foes.

PSALM 60:12

When the ways of people please the LORD, he makes even their enemies live at peace with them.

PROVERBS 16:7

Fearing people is a dangerous trap, but to trust the LORD means safety.

PROVERBS 29:25

If people persecute you because you are a Christian, don't curse them; pray that God will bless them.

Do what the Scriptures say: "If your enemies are hungry, feed them. If they are thirsty, give them something to drink, and they will be ashamed of what they have done to you."

ROMANS 12:14, 20

You have heard that the law of Moses says, "Love your neighbor" and hate your enemy. But I say, love your enemies! Pray for those who persecute you! In that way, you will be acting as true children of your Father in heaven. For he gives his sunlight to both the evil and the good, and he sends rain on the just and on the unjust, too. If you love only those who love you, what good is that? Even corrupt tax collectors do that much. If you are kind only to your friends, how are you different from anyone else? Even pagans do that. But you are to be perfect, even as your Father in heaven is perfect.

MATTHEW 5:43-48

See also Forgiving Others, Hate, Mercy.

Eternal Life

Loving and obeying God will not necessarily make us rich, handsome, or successful—not by this world's standards, anyway. In fact, the Bible actually promises that we will have to endure some scorn for holding fast to God. The world sneers at people who believe that the next life is so good that the present life can't begin to compare with it.

Too bad we often neglect this belief. The Bible certainly doesn't.

> You will not leave my soul among the dead or allow your godly one to rot in the grave. You will show me the way of life, granting me the joy of your presence and the pleasures of living with you forever.
>
> PSALM 16:10-11

> I know that my Redeemer lives, and that he will stand upon the earth at last. And after my body has decayed, yet in my body I will see God! I will see him for myself. Yes, I will see him with my own eyes. I am overwhelmed at the thought!
>
> JOB 19:25-27

> Humans can reproduce only human life, but the Holy Spirit gives new life from heaven.
> All who believe in God's Son have eternal life. Those who don't obey the Son will never experience eternal life, but the wrath of God remains upon them.
>
> JOHN 3:6, 36

This is the will of God, that I should not lose even one of all those he has given me, but that I should raise them to eternal life at the last day. For it is my Father's will that all who see his Son and believe in him should have eternal life—that I should raise them at the last day.

JOHN 6:39-40

I assure you, anyone who obeys my teaching will never die!
JOHN 8:51

If we have hope in Christ only for this life, we are the most miserable people in the world.

But the fact is that Christ has been raised from the dead. He has become the first of a great harvest of those who will be raised to life again.

So you see, just as death came into the world through a man, Adam, now the resurrection from the dead has begun through another man, Christ. Everyone dies because all of us are related to Adam, the first man. But all who are related to Christ, the other man, will be given new life.

1 CORINTHIANS 15:19-22

The wages of sin is death, but the free gift of God is eternal life through Christ Jesus our Lord.

ROMANS 6:23

The Spirit of God, who raised Jesus from the dead, lives in you. And just as he raised Christ from the dead, he will give life to your mortal body by this same Spirit living within you.

ROMANS 8:11

Let me tell you a wonderful secret God has revealed to us. Not all of us will die, but we will all be transformed. It will happen in a moment, in the blinking of an eye, when the last trumpet is blown. For when the trumpet sounds, the Christians who have died will be raised with transformed bodies.

And then we who are living will be transformed so that we will never die. For our perishable earthly bodies must be transformed into heavenly bodies that will never die.

When this happens—when our perishable earthly bodies have been transformed into heavenly bodies that will never die—then at last the Scriptures will come true: "Death is swallowed up in victory. O death, where is your victory? O death, where is your sting?"

1 CORINTHIANS 15:51-55

Dear brothers and sisters, work hard to prove that you really are among those God has called and chosen. Doing this, you will never stumble or fall away. And God will open wide the gates of heaven for you to enter into the eternal Kingdom of our Lord and Savior Jesus Christ.

2 PETER 1:10-11

I heard a loud shout from the throne, saying, "Look, the home of God is now among his people! He will live with them, and they will be his people. God himself will be with them. He will remove all of their sorrows, and there will be no more death or sorrow or crying or pain. For the old world and its evils are gone forever."

And the one sitting on the throne said, "Look, I am making all things new!"

REVELATION 21:3-5

See also Death, Heaven, Hell, Jesus' Second Coming.

Faith

Martin Luther defined faith as "a living, daring confidence in God's grace." It is such an important element in the Christian life that we refer to our walk with God as "the life of faith," and we refer to our beliefs as "the faith." Faith goes well beyond mental beliefs and ideas. After all, as Luther said, it is "living, daring." More than a "head thing," it is a "heart thing" and a "will thing."

One of the greatest promises made in the Bible is Jesus' assurance that we do not need to be "giants of the faith" to please God. Even a little faith is a good thing—and powerful, too. Small faith can always grow.

I assure you, even if you had faith as small as a mustard seed you could say to this mountain, "Move from here to there," and it would move. Nothing would be impossible.

MATTHEW 17:20

Accept Christians who are weak in faith, and don't argue with them about what they think is right or wrong.

ROMANS 14:1

There are three things that will endure—faith, hope, and love.

1 CORINTHIANS 13:13

We live by believing and not by seeing.

2 CORINTHIANS 5:7

I myself no longer live, but Christ lives in me. So I live my life in this earthly body by trusting in the Son of God, who loved me and gave himself for me.

GALATIANS 2:20

I pray that Christ will be more and more at home in your hearts as you trust in him. May your roots go down deep into the soil of God's marvelous love. And may you have the power to understand, as all God's people should, how wide, how long, how high, and how deep his love really is. May you experience the love of Christ, though it is so great you will never fully understand it. Then you will be filled with the fullness of life and power that comes from God.

EPHESIANS 3:17-19

Just as you accepted Christ Jesus as your Lord, you must continue to live in obedience to him. Let your roots grow down into him and draw up nourishment from him, so you will grow in faith, strong and vigorous in the truth you were taught. Let your lives overflow with thanksgiving for all he has done.

COLOSSIANS 2:6-7

Every child of God defeats this evil world by trusting Christ to give the victory. And the ones who win this battle against the world are the ones who believe that Jesus is the Son of God.

1 JOHN 5:4

Dear brothers and sisters, what's the use of saying you have faith if you don't prove it by your actions? That kind of faith can't save anyone. Suppose you see a brother or sister who needs food or clothing, and you say, "Well, good-bye and God bless you; stay warm and eat well"—but then you don't give that person any food or clothing. What good does that do?

So you see, it isn't enough just to have faith. Faith that doesn't show itself by good deeds is no faith at all—it is dead and useless.

Now someone may argue, "Some people have faith; others have good deeds." . . . Fool! When will you ever learn that faith that does not result in good deeds is useless?

JAMES 2:14-20

See also Hope, Trusting God.

Fear

Franklin D. Roosevelt assured people that "the only thing we have to fear is fear itself." The Bible makes an even bolder promise: We have *nothing* to fear, period.

This doesn't mean our life will be trouble-free—far from it. But the message of God's Word is that fear—of enemies, of the future, of failure, whatever—need not dominate our life and paralyze us.

> *Even when I walk through the dark valley of death, I will not be afraid, for you are close beside me. Your rod and your staff protect and comfort me.*
>
> *You prepare a feast for me in the presence of my enemies. You welcome me as a guest, anointing my head with oil. My cup overflows with blessings.*
>
> PSALM 23:4-5

> *The LORD is my light and my salvation—so why should I be afraid? The LORD protects me from danger—so why should I tremble?*
>
> *When evil people come to destroy me, when my enemies and foes attack me, they will stumble and fall. Though a mighty army surrounds me, my heart will know no fear. Even if they attack me, I remain confident.*
>
> PSALM 27:1-3

> *God is our refuge and strength, always ready to help in times of trouble. So we will not fear, even if earthquakes come and the mountains crumble into the sea. Let the oceans roar and foam. Let the mountains tremble as the waters surge!*
>
> *A river brings joy to the city of our God, the sacred home of*

the Most High. God himself lives in that city; it cannot be destroyed.

PSALM 46:1-5

Fearing people is a dangerous trap, but to trust the LORD means safety.

PROVERBS 29:25

Don't be afraid, for I am with you. Do not be dismayed, for I am your God. I will strengthen you. I will help you. I will uphold you with my victorious right hand.

See, all your angry enemies lie there, confused and ashamed. Anyone who opposes you will die. You will look for them in vain. They will all be gone! I am holding you by your right hand—I, the LORD your God. And I say to you, "Do not be afraid. I am here to help you."

ISAIAH 41:10-13

Sorrow and mourning will disappear, and they will be overcome with joy and gladness.

I, even I, am the one who comforts you. So why are you afraid of mere humans, who wither like the grass and disappear?

ISAIAH 51:11-12

Don't be afraid of those who want to kill you. They can only kill your body; they cannot touch your soul. Fear only God, who can destroy both soul and body in hell.

MATTHEW 10:28

I am leaving you with a gift—peace of mind and heart. And the peace I give isn't like the peace the world gives. So don't be troubled or afraid.

JOHN 14:27

No, despite all these things, overwhelming victory is ours through Christ, who loved us.

And I am convinced that nothing can ever separate us from his love. Death can't, and life can't. The angels can't, and the demons can't. Our fears for today, our worries about tomorrow, and even the powers of hell can't keep God's love away. Whether we are high above the sky or in the deepest ocean, nothing in all creation will ever be able to separate us from the love of God that is revealed in Christ Jesus our Lord.

ROMANS 8:37-39

See also Contentment, Hope, Worry and Anxiety.

Fellowship with God

The Bible reminds us again and again that God is a *personal* God—not some faraway, distant idea, but the Supreme Person, who actually enjoys the fellowship of his people. Unlike some of the cold, unapproachable gods of some religions, our God is approachable. He wants to be near us, and he wants our devotion and love.

The good news is that we don't have to wait for death to enjoy this. Fellowship with God begins now, and it continues forever and ever without end.

> *I will walk among you; I will be your God, and you will be my people.*
>
> LEVITICUS 26:12

> *We are telling you about what we ourselves have actually seen and heard, so that you may have fellowship with us. And our fellowship is with the Father and with his Son, Jesus Christ.*
>
> *This is the message he has given us to announce to you: God is light and there is no darkness in him at all. So we are lying if we say we have fellowship with God but go on living in spiritual darkness. We are not living in the truth. But if we are living in the light of God's presence, just as Christ is, then we have fellowship with each other, and the blood of Jesus, his Son, cleanses us from every sin.*
>
> 1 JOHN 1:3, 5-7

Those who obey God's commandments live in fellowship with him, and he with them. And we know he lives in us because the Holy Spirit lives in us.

1 JOHN 3:24

Where two or three gather together because they are mine, I am there among them.

MATTHEW 18:20

Since Christ lives within you, even though your body will die because of sin, your spirit is alive because you have been made right with God. And since we are his children, we will share his treasures—for everything God gives to his Son, Christ, is ours, too. But if we are to share his glory, we must also share his suffering.

ROMANS 8:10, 17

If you wander beyond the teaching of Christ, you will not have fellowship with God. But if you continue in the teaching of Christ, you will have fellowship with both the Father and the Son.

2 JOHN 1:9

Look! Here I stand at the door and knock. If you hear me calling and open the door, I will come in, and we will share a meal as friends.

REVELATION 3:20

I heard a loud shout from the throne, saying, "Look, the home of God is now among his people! He will live with them, and they will be his people. God himself will be with them. He will remove all of their sorrows, and there will be no more death or sorrow or crying or pain. For the old world and its evils are gone forever."

REVELATION 21:3-4

See also Eternal Life, Heaven, Loneliness, Prayer.

Forgiving Others

Probably one of the most quoted lines of poetry is Alexander Pope's "To err is human, to forgive divine." Pope caught the essence of the Bible's message. God forgives us, and if we are his people, his children, we must be forgiving also. There is no way around this. Grudges have no place in the Christian life. Just as we desperately need God's forgiveness of our failings, so we desperately need to forgive those who fail us.

> *People with good sense restrain their anger; they earn esteem by overlooking wrongs.*
>
> PROVERBS 19:11

> *Don't say, "I will get even for this wrong." Wait for the LORD to handle the matter.*
>
> PROVERBS 20:22

> *God blesses those who are merciful, for they will be shown mercy.*
>
> *Don't resist an evil person! If you are slapped on the right cheek, turn the other, too. If you are ordered to court and your shirt is taken from you, give your coat, too. If a soldier demands that you carry his gear for a mile, carry it two miles. Give to those who ask, and don't turn away from those who want to borrow.*
>
> *You have heard that the law of Moses says, "Love your neighbor" and hate your enemy. But I say, love your enemies! Pray for those who persecute you! In that way, you will be acting as true children of your Father in heaven. For he gives his sunlight to both the evil and the good, and he sends rain on*

the just and on the unjust, too. If you love only those who love you, what good is that? Even corrupt tax collectors do that much. If you are kind only to your friends, how are you different from anyone else? Even pagans do that.

MATTHEW 5:7, 39-47

If you forgive those who sin against you, your heavenly Father will forgive you. But if you refuse to forgive others, your Father will not forgive your sins.

MATTHEW 6:14-15

You must make allowance for each other's faults and forgive the person who offends you. Remember, the Lord forgave you, so you must forgive others.

COLOSSIANS 3:13

I am warning you! If another believer sins, rebuke him; then if he repents, forgive him. Even if he wrongs you seven times a day and each time turns again and asks forgiveness, forgive him.

LUKE 17:3-4

See also Anger, Enemies, Mercy, Revenge.

Friends

If loneliness is a problem in the modern world (and it definitely is), friendship ought to be highly valued. It is, but there's the problem of the "loyalty gap," the feeling that relationships—marriage, friendship, employer/employee—are temporary at best, to be dissolved whenever one party feels like it. This situation isn't new, as the Bible makes clear.

> *Many will say they are loyal friends, but who can find one who is really faithful?*
>
> PROVERBS 20:6

Of course, the Bible gives some great examples of "really faithful" friends. The classic example is that Old Testament pair, David and Jonathan.

> *After David had finished talking with Saul, he met Jonathan, the king's son. There was an immediate bond of love between them, and they became the best of friends. . . . And Jonathan made a special vow to be David's friend, and he sealed the pact by giving him his robe, tunic, sword, bow, and belt.*
>
> 1 SAMUEL 18:1-4

The book of Proverbs is, in some ways, the book of friendship, with wise words about the true meaning of genuine friendship.

> *A friend is always loyal, and a brother is born to help in time of need.*
>
> PROVERBS 17:17

There are "friends" who destroy each other, but a real friend sticks closer than a brother.

PROVERBS 18:24

A troublemaker plants seeds of strife; gossip separates the best of friends.

PROVERBS 16:28

Disregarding another person's faults preserves love; telling about them separates close friends.

PROVERBS 17:9

It's harder to make amends with an offended friend than to capture a fortified city. Arguments separate friends like a gate locked with iron bars.

PROVERBS 18:19

Just as damaging as a mad man shooting a lethal weapon is someone who lies to a friend and then says, "I was only joking."

PROVERBS 26:18-19

The godly give good advice to their friends; the wicked lead them astray.

PROVERBS 12:26

Keep away from angry, short-tempered people, or you will learn to be like them and endanger your soul.

PROVERBS 22:24-25

Wicked people are an abomination to the LORD, but he offers his friendship to the godly.

PROVERBS 3:32

We know what real love is because Christ gave up his life for us. And so we also ought to give up our lives for our Christian brothers and sisters.

1 JOHN 3:16

Continue to love each other with true Christian love. Don't forget to show hospitality to strangers, for some who have done this have entertained angels without realizing it! Don't forget about those in prison. Suffer with them as though you were there yourself. Share the sorrow of those being mistreated, as though you feel their pain in your own bodies.

HEBREWS 13:1-3

Dear brothers and sisters, what's the use of saying you have faith if you don't prove it by your actions? That kind of faith can't save anyone. Suppose you see a brother or sister who needs food or clothing, and you say, "Well, good-bye and God bless you; stay warm and eat well"—but then you don't give that person any food or clothing. What good does that do?

So you see, it isn't enough just to have faith. Faith that doesn't show itself by good deeds is no faith at all—it is dead and useless.

JAMES 2:14-17

See also Fellowship with God, Loneliness.

God's Love for Us

Love is such an overused word. Don't we "love" hot dogs and apple pie and "love" going to the beach? But love in the Bible has a much richer meaning, particularly when applied to God's feeling toward his people. The Bible describes a kind of love that goes far beyond the greatest human capacity.

> *The LORD watches over those who fear him, those who rely on his unfailing love.*
>
> *We depend on the LORD alone to save us. Only he can help us, protecting us like a shield.*
>
> PSALM 33:18, 20

> *I have loved you, my people, with an everlasting love. With unfailing love I have drawn you to myself.*
>
> JEREMIAH 31:3

> *Many sorrows come to the wicked, but unfailing love surrounds those who trust the LORD. So rejoice in the LORD and be glad, all you who obey him! Shout for joy, all you whose hearts are pure!*
>
> PSALM 32:10-11

> *The Word became human and lived here on earth among us. He was full of unfailing love and faithfulness. And we have seen his glory, the glory of the only Son of the Father.*
>
> JOHN 1:14

God so loved the world that he gave his only Son, so that everyone who believes in him will not perish but have eternal life. God did not send his Son into the world to condemn it, but to save it.

JOHN 3:16-17

We know how dearly God loves us, because he has given us the Holy Spirit to fill our hearts with his love.

But God showed his great love for us by sending Christ to die for us while we were still sinners. And since we have been made right in God's sight by the blood of Christ, he will certainly save us from God's judgment. For since we were restored to friendship with God by the death of his Son while we were still his enemies, we will certainly be delivered from eternal punishment by his life. So now we can rejoice in our wonderful new relationship with God—all because of what our Lord Jesus Christ has done for us in making us friends of God.

ROMANS 5:5, 8-11

We know that God causes everything to work together for the good of those who love God and are called according to his purpose for them.

ROMANS 8:28

God is so rich in mercy, and he loved us so very much, that even while we were dead because of our sins, he gave us life when he raised Christ from the dead. (It is only by God's special favor that you have been saved!) For he raised us from the dead along with Christ, and we are seated with him in the heavenly realms—all because we are one with Christ Jesus. And so God can always point to us as examples of the incredible wealth of his favor and kindness toward us, as shown in all he has done for us through Christ Jesus.

EPHESIANS 2:4-7

May you experience the love of Christ, though it is so great you will never fully understand it. Then you will be filled with the fullness of life and power that comes from God.

EPHESIANS 3:19

Anyone who does not love does not know God—for God is love.

God showed how much he loved us by sending his only Son into the world so that we might have eternal life through him. This is real love. It is not that we loved God, but that he loved us and sent his Son as a sacrifice to take away our sins.

Dear friends, since God loved us that much, we surely ought to love each other. No one has ever seen God. But if we love each other, God lives in us, and his love has been brought to full expression through us.

And God has given us his Spirit as proof that we live in him and he in us.

1 JOHN 4:8-13

See also Comfort in Times of Trouble, Discipline and Correction.

God's Mercy

"Don't get mad—get even." This seems to be the usual way people view the world nowadays. We should be thankful that God takes a different view of things. Although the Bible makes it clear that God is the great Judge who hates all evildoing, he is also the merciful God who forgives and accepts people who turn to him.

> Give thanks to the LORD, for he is good! His faithful love endures forever.
>
> 1 CHRONICLES 16:34

> Let the people turn from their wicked deeds. Let them banish from their minds the very thought of doing wrong! Let them turn to the LORD that he may have mercy on them. Yes, turn to our God, for he will abundantly pardon.
>
> ISAIAH 55:7

> As surely as I live, says the Sovereign LORD, I take no pleasure in the death of wicked people. I only want them to turn from their wicked ways so they can live. Turn! Turn from your wickedness, O people of Israel! Why should you die?
>
> EZEKIEL 33:11

> God is so rich in mercy, and he loved us so very much, that even while we were dead because of our sins, he gave us life when he raised Christ from the dead. (It is only by God's special favor that you have been saved!) For he raised us from the dead along with Christ, and we are seated with him in the heavenly realms—all because we are one with Christ Jesus.
>
> EPHESIANS 2:4-6

Where is another God like you, who pardons the sins of the survivors among his people? You cannot stay angry with your people forever, because you delight in showing mercy. Once again you will have compassion on us. You will trample our sins under your feet and throw them into the depths of the ocean!

MICAH 7:18-19

If a shepherd has one hundred sheep, and one wanders away and is lost, what will he do? Won't he leave the ninety-nine others and go out into the hills to search for the lost one? And if he finds it, he will surely rejoice over it more than over the ninety-nine that didn't wander away! In the same way, it is not my heavenly Father's will that even one of these little ones should perish.

MATTHEW 18:12-14

Now turn from your sins and turn to God, so you can be cleansed of your sins. Then wonderful times of refreshment will come from the presence of the Lord, and he will send Jesus your Messiah to you again.

ACTS 3:19-20

He saved us, not because of the good things we did, but because of his mercy. He washed away our sins and gave us a new life through the Holy Spirit.

TITUS 3:5

Let us come boldly to the throne of our gracious God. There we will receive his mercy, and we will find grace to help us when we need it.

HEBREWS 4:16

See also Confessing Sin, Guilt, Repentance.

Guilt

Many psychologists like to talk about—and try to get rid of—patients' guilt feelings. They often assume that the *feeling* is the problem. If it can be gotten rid of, the problem is solved—or so they say. They overlook the fact that people often experience genuine guilt over having wronged someone—another person or God himself. Getting rid of the *feeling* isn't the solution then, is it? The problem is that a precious relationship has been broken. It needs to be mended, not psychoanalyzed away.

Happily, the Bible holds out more promise than most of these so-called experts. It assures us that much of our guilt isn't just a feeling—it is a real awareness of harm done to someone. It also assures us that God is willing and eager to forgive us, cleanse us of guilt, and restore joy to our life.

> O God, you know how foolish I am; my sins cannot be hidden from you.
>
> PSALM 69:5

> He has not punished us for all our sins, nor does he deal with us as we deserve. For his unfailing love toward those who fear him is as great as the height of the heavens above the earth. He has removed our rebellious acts as far away from us as the east is from the west. The LORD is like a father to his children, tender and compassionate to those who fear him. For he understands how weak we are; he knows we are only dust.
>
> PSALM 103:10-14

Let the people turn from their wicked deeds. Let them banish from their minds the very thought of doing wrong! Let them turn to the LORD that he may have mercy on them. Yes, turn to our God, for he will abundantly pardon.

ISAIAH 55:7

All have sinned; all fall short of God's glorious standard. Yet now God in his gracious kindness declares us not guilty. He has done this through Christ Jesus, who has freed us by taking away our sins.

ROMANS 3:23-24

If we are living in the light of God's presence, just as Christ is, then we have fellowship with each other, and the blood of Jesus, his Son, cleanses us from every sin.

1 JOHN 1:7

See also Confessing Sin, God's Mercy, Repentance, Sin and Redemption.

Hate

Turn on the daily news, and you can't help but notice how hate-filled the world is. One nation against another, one ethnic group hating another, one political group spouting hateful half-truths about another. You could easily get the impression that some people actually *enjoy* hating others. The more aware we are of this, the more normal it seems. Whatever happened to the old saying, "Don't hate people—hate their *ways*"?

The Bible has one basic word regarding hatred of people: *don't.*

> Hatred stirs up quarrels, but love covers all offenses.
>
> PROVERBS 10:12

> You have heard that the law of Moses says, "Love your neighbor" and hate your enemy. But I say, love your enemies! Pray for those who persecute you! In that way, you will be acting as true children of your Father in heaven. For he gives his sunlight to both the evil and the good, and he sends rain on the just and on the unjust, too.
>
> MATTHEW 5:43-45

> If anyone says, "I am living in the light," but hates a Christian brother or sister, that person is still living in darkness. Anyone who loves other Christians is living in the light and does not cause anyone to stumble. Anyone who hates a Christian brother or sister is living and walking in darkness. Such a person is lost, having been blinded by the darkness.
>
> 1 JOHN 2:9-11

If someone says, "I love God," but hates a Christian brother or sister, that person is a liar; for if we don't love people we can see, how can we love God, whom we have not seen? And God himself has commanded that we must love not only him but our Christian brothers and sisters, too.

1 JOHN 4:20-21

See also Anger, Enemies, Forgiving Others, Mercy.

Heaven

Christians are often stereotyped as constantly preaching about the fires of hell, but many preachers have also focused on heaven—God's rest and joy and complete satisfaction for us after enduring the troubles of this earthly life. It is mentioned again and again in the New Testament, not as an afterthought but as a key element in Christian belief. C. S. Lewis observed that belief in heaven is "not a form of escapism or wishful thinking, but one of the things a Christian is meant to do."

Does being otherworldly mean we are of no use in this life? Hardly. Lewis also noted that Christians who had a genuine belief in the joys of heaven seemed to be the happiest people here on earth—and also the most likely to make the earth a more livable place.

> *I know that my Redeemer lives, and that he will stand upon the earth at last. And after my body has decayed, yet in my body I will see God! I will see him for myself. Yes, I will see him with my own eyes. I am overwhelmed at the thought!*
>
> JOB 19:25-27

> *Surely your goodness and unfailing love will pursue me all the days of my life, and I will live in the house of the LORD forever.*
>
> PSALM 23:6

If we have hope in Christ only for this life, we are the most miserable people in the world.

But the fact is that Christ has been raised from the dead. He has become the first of a great harvest of those who will be raised to life again.

1 CORINTHIANS 15:19-20

I give them eternal life, and they will never perish. No one will snatch them away from me, for my Father has given them to me, and he is more powerful than anyone else. So no one can take them from me.

JOHN 10:28-29

There are many rooms in my Father's home, and I am going to prepare a place for you. If this were not so, I would tell you plainly. When everything is ready, I will come and get you, so that you will always be with me where I am.

JOHN 14:2-3

We are citizens of heaven, where the Lord Jesus Christ lives. And we are eagerly waiting for him to return as our Savior. He will take these weak mortal bodies of ours and change them into glorious bodies like his own, using the same mighty power that he will use to conquer everything, everywhere.

PHILIPPIANS 3:20-21

Since you have been raised to new life with Christ, set your sights on the realities of heaven, where Christ sits at God's right hand in the place of honor and power. Let heaven fill your thoughts. Do not think only about things down here on earth. For you died when Christ died, and your real life is hidden with Christ in God. And when Christ, who is your real life, is revealed to the whole world, you will share in all his glory.

COLOSSIANS 3:1-4

The Lord will deliver me from every evil attack and will bring me safely to his heavenly Kingdom. To God be the glory forever and ever. Amen.

2 TIMOTHY 4:18

This world is not our home; we are looking forward to our city in heaven, which is yet to come.

HEBREWS 13:14

We live with a wonderful expectation because Jesus Christ rose again from the dead. For God has reserved a priceless inheritance for his children. It is kept in heaven for you, pure and undefiled.

1 PETER 1:3-4

Anyone who is willing to hear should listen to the Spirit and understand what the Spirit is saying to the churches. Everyone who is victorious will eat from the tree of life in the paradise of God.

REVELATION 2:7

See also Eternal Life, Hell, Jesus' Second Coming.

Hell

Now here is an unpopular topic, one that even very faithful people tend to avoid. In our age when nothing seems permanent, the idea of being permanently separated from God strikes people as too—well, *final*. We wonder, *Shouldn't there be, perhaps, a second chance?* No wonder belief in reincarnation is so popular. It gives people the comfort of believing that if they ruin this life, they will get another chance, and another, and . . .

This isn't the picture the Bible presents. It presents us with one life per person, a life that can be used in the service and worship of God—or that can be lived without God. God made us free, able to make moral and spiritual choices. So he can't really be accused of "sending people to hell," as if he took some delight in punishing us. Far from it! But since we are free, we *can*—finally and forever—say no to God.

> As surely as I live, says the Sovereign LORD, I take no pleasure in the death of wicked people. I only want them to turn from their wicked ways so they can live. Turn! Turn from your wickedness, O people of Israel! Why should you die?
>
> EZEKIEL 33:11

> You can enter God's Kingdom only through the narrow gate. The highway to hell is broad, and its gate is wide for the many who choose the easy way. But the gateway to life is small, and the road is narrow, and only a few ever find it.
>
> MATTHEW 7:13-14

> I, the Son of Man, will send my angels, and they will

remove from my Kingdom everything that causes sin and all
who do evil, and they will throw them into the furnace and
burn them. There will be weeping and gnashing of teeth.
Then the godly will shine like the sun in their Father's Kingdom. Anyone who is willing to hear should listen and understand!

MATTHEW 13:41-43

The Kingdom of Heaven is like a fishing net that is thrown
into the water and gathers fish of every kind. When the net is
full, they drag it up onto the shore, sit down, sort the good
fish into crates, and throw the bad ones away. That is the
way it will be at the end of the world. The angels will come
and separate the wicked people from the godly, throwing the
wicked into the fire. There will be weeping and gnashing of
teeth.

MATTHEW 13:47-50

Cowards who turn away from me, and unbelievers, and the
corrupt, and murderers, and the immoral, and those who
practice witchcraft, and idol worshipers, and all liars—their
doom is in the lake that burns with fire and sulfur. This is the
second death.

REVELATION 21:8

See also Eternal Life, Heaven, Jesus' Second Coming.

The Holy Spirit

Recent years have seen a renewed interest in the Holy Spirit, and rightly so. For too long the Spirit was a neglected part of our belief, something people tacked on to their creed (". . . and I believe in the Holy Spirit"). Christians around the globe have gone back to the Bible and concluded that whoever does not know the Spirit does not know God at all.

We have devoted a separate topic to the baptism of the Spirit/gifts of the Spirit, but as you will see from the Bible promises under this topic, the Spirit himself *is* God's great gift to all believers.

> I will pour out my Spirit upon all people. Your sons and daughters will prophesy. Your old men will dream dreams. Your young men will see visions. In those days, I will pour out my Spirit even on servants, men and women alike.
>
> JOEL 2:28-29

> [John the Baptist:] "I baptize with water those who turn from their sins and turn to God. But someone is coming soon who is far greater than I am—so much greater that I am not even worthy to be his slave. He will baptize you with the Holy Spirit and with fire."
>
> MATTHEW 3:11

> Those who speak against the Son of Man may be forgiven, but anyone who speaks blasphemies against the Holy Spirit will never be forgiven.
>
> LUKE 12:10

The truth is, no one can enter the Kingdom of God without being born of water and the Spirit. Humans can reproduce only human life, but the Holy Spirit gives new life from heaven.

JOHN 3:5-6

I will ask the Father, and he will give you another Counselor, who will never leave you. He is the Holy Spirit, who leads into all truth. The world at large cannot receive him, because it isn't looking for him and doesn't recognize him. But you do, because he lives with you now and later will be in you.

But when the Father sends the Counselor as my representative—and by the Counselor I mean the Holy Spirit—he will teach you everything and will remind you of everything I myself have told you.

JOHN 14:16-17, 26

When the Spirit of truth comes, he will guide you into all truth. He will not be presenting his own ideas; he will be telling you what he has heard. He will tell you about the future. He will bring me glory by revealing to you whatever he receives from me. All that the Father has is mine; this is what I mean when I say that the Spirit will reveal to you whatever he receives from me.

JOHN 16:13-15

When the Holy Spirit has come upon you, you will receive power and will tell people about me everywhere—in Jerusalem, throughout Judea, in Samaria, and to the ends of the earth.

ACTS 1:8

Suddenly, there was a sound from heaven like the roaring of a mighty windstorm in the skies above them, and it filled the house where they were meeting. Then, what looked like flames or tongues of fire appeared and settled on each of them. And everyone present was filled with the Holy Spirit and began speaking in other tongues, as the Holy Spirit gave them this ability.

ACTS 2:2-4

We know how dearly God loves us, because he has given us the Holy Spirit to fill our hearts with his love.

ROMANS 5:5

The power of the life-giving Spirit has freed you through Christ Jesus from the power of sin that leads to death.

Those who are dominated by the sinful nature think about sinful things, but those who are controlled by the Holy Spirit think about things that please the Spirit. If your sinful nature controls your mind, there is death. But if the Holy Spirit controls your mind, there is life and peace.

The Spirit of God, who raised Jesus from the dead, lives in you. And just as he raised Christ from the dead, he will give life to your mortal body by this same Spirit living within you.

For all who are led by the Spirit of God are children of God.

So you should not be like cowering, fearful slaves. You should behave instead like God's very own children, adopted into his family—calling him "Father, dear Father." For his Holy Spirit speaks to us deep in our hearts and tells us that we are God's children.

ROMANS 8:2, 5-6, 11, 14-16

He saved us, not because of the good things we did, but because of his mercy. He washed away our sins and gave us a new life through the Holy Spirit. He generously poured out the Spirit upon us because of what Jesus Christ our Savior did.

TITUS 3:5-6

Those who obey God's commandments live in fellowship with him, and he with them. And we know he lives in us because the Holy Spirit lives in us.

1 JOHN 3:24

See also Baptism of the Spirit/Gifts of the Spirit.

Hope

"High Hopes" could be the subtitle of the Bible, the New Testament in particular. The Bible authors understood that people aren't content to merely live but need to have something to live *for*. It is human to wonder about the future, for God made us that way. Happily, he gave many promises of a blessed future to those who follow him.

Why am I discouraged? Why so sad? I will put my hope in God! I will praise him again—my Savior and my God!

PSALM 42:11

The hopes of the godly result in happiness, but the expectations of the wicked are all in vain.

PROVERBS 10:28

Love the LORD, all you faithful ones! For the LORD protects those who are loyal to him, but he harshly punishes all who are arrogant. So be strong and take courage, all you who put your hope in the LORD!

PSALM 31:23-24

The LORD watches over those who fear him, those who rely on his unfailing love.

PSALM 33:18

Hope deferred makes the heart sick, but when dreams come true, there is life and joy.

PROVERBS 13:12

Blessed are those who trust in the LORD and have made the LORD their hope and confidence.

JEREMIAH 17:7

Such things were written in the Scriptures long ago to teach us. They give us hope and encouragement as we wait patiently for God's promises.

ROMANS 15:4

There are three things that will endure—faith, hope, and love.

1 CORINTHIANS 13:13

We who live by the Spirit eagerly wait to receive everything promised to us who are right with God through faith.

GALATIANS 5:5

In those days you were living apart from Christ. You were excluded from God's people, Israel, and you did not know the promises God had made to them. You lived in this world without God and without hope. But now you belong to Christ Jesus. Though you once were far away from God, now you have been brought near to him because of the blood of Christ.

EPHESIANS 2:12-13

This is the secret: Christ lives in you, and this is your assurance that you will share in his glory.

COLOSSIANS 1:27

Brothers and sisters, I want you to know what will happen to the Christians who have died so you will not be full of sorrow like people who have no hope. For since we believe that Jesus died and was raised to life again, we also believe that when Jesus comes, God will bring back with Jesus all the Christians who have died.

1 THESSALONIANS 4:13-14

*He declared us not guilty because of his great kindness. And
now we know that we will inherit eternal life.*

TITUS 3:7

*God has given us both his promise and his oath. These two
things are unchangeable because it is impossible for God to
lie. Therefore, we who have fled to him for refuge can take
new courage, for we can hold on to his promise with confidence.*

*This confidence is like a strong and trustworthy anchor for
our souls. It leads us through the curtain of heaven into God's
inner sanctuary.*

HEBREWS 6:18-19

*Without wavering, let us hold tightly to the hope we say we
have, for God can be trusted to keep his promise.*

HEBREWS 10:23

*What is faith? It is the confident assurance that what we
hope for is going to happen. It is the evidence of things we
cannot yet see.*

HEBREWS 11:1

*All honor to the God and Father of our Lord Jesus Christ, for
it is by his boundless mercy that God has given us the privilege
of being born again. Now we live with a wonderful expectation because Jesus Christ rose again from the dead. For God
has reserved a priceless inheritance for his children. It is kept in
heaven for you, pure and undefiled, beyond the reach of
change and decay. And God, in his mighty power, will protect
you until you receive this salvation, because you are trusting
him. It will be revealed on the last day for all to see. So be
truly glad! There is wonderful joy ahead, even though it is necessary for you to endure many trials for a while.*

1 PETER 1:3-6

See also Eternal Life, Faith, Heaven, Trusting God.

Hypocrisy

An old joke about hypocrites involves someone who said, "I don't go to church. Churches are full of hypocrites." The punch line was, "Come on in; there's always room for one more!"

While there is no doubt that there are hypocrites in the church, there is no place for them in the Kingdom. God's promises are for believers, not for those who only pretend to believe. Some of the harshest warnings in the Bible are reserved for the pretenders in religion, the ones who act out a life of faith but inwardly deny it.

> *Smooth words may hide a wicked heart, just as a pretty glaze covers a common clay pot.*
>
> *People with hate in their hearts may sound pleasant enough, but don't believe them. Though they pretend to be kind, their hearts are full of all kinds of evil. While their hatred may be concealed by trickery, it will finally come to light for all to see.*
>
> PROVERBS 26:23-26

> *I will not allow deceivers to serve me, and liars will not be allowed to enter my presence.*
>
> PSALM 101:7

> *I [God] hate all your show and pretense—the hypocrisy of your religious festivals and solemn assemblies. I will not accept your burnt offerings and grain offerings. I won't even notice all your choice peace offerings. Away with your hymns of praise! They are only noise to my ears. I will not listen to your music, no matter how lovely it is. Instead, I*

want to see a mighty flood of justice, a river of righteous living that will never run dry.

AMOS 5:21-24

Take care! Don't do your good deeds publicly, to be admired, because then you will lose the reward from your Father in heaven. When you give a gift to someone in need, don't shout about it as the hypocrites do—blowing trumpets in the synagogues and streets to call attention to their acts of charity! I assure you, they have received all the reward they will ever get. But when you give to someone, don't tell your left hand what your right hand is doing.

And now about prayer. When you pray, don't be like the hypocrites who love to pray publicly on street corners and in the synagogues where everyone can see them. I assure you, that is all the reward they will ever get.

And when you fast, don't make it obvious, as the hypocrites do, who try to look pale and disheveled so people will admire them for their fasting. I assure you, that is the only reward they will ever get.

MATTHEW 6:1-3, 5, 16

Why worry about a speck in your friend's eye when you have a log in your own? How can you think of saying, "Let me help you get rid of that speck in your eye," when you can't see past the log in your own eye? Hypocrite! First get rid of the log from your own eye; then perhaps you will see well enough to deal with the speck in your friend's eye.

MATTHEW 7:3-5

The time is coming when everything will be revealed; all that is secret will be made public. Whatever you have said in the dark will be heard in the light, and what you have whispered behind closed doors will be shouted from the housetops for all to hear!

LUKE 12:2-3

Why do you call me "Lord," when you won't obey me?

LUKE 6:46

If someone says, "I belong to God," but doesn't obey God's commandments, that person is a liar and does not live in the truth.

1 JOHN 2:4

Remember, it is a message to obey, not just to listen to. If you don't obey, you are only fooling yourself. For if you just listen and don't obey, it is like looking at your face in a mirror but doing nothing to improve your appearance. You see yourself, walk away, and forget what you look like. But if you keep looking steadily into God's perfect law—the law that sets you free—and if you do what it says and don't forget what you heard, then God will bless you for doing it.

If you claim to be religious but don't control your tongue, you are just fooling yourself, and your religion is worthless. Pure and lasting religion in the sight of God our Father means that we must care for orphans and widows in their troubles, and refuse to let the world corrupt us.

JAMES 1:22-27

See also Judging Others.

Jesus' Second Coming

You don't hear so much talk about heaven anymore or about when Jesus will return in glory. Too many believers nowadays forget how much the Bible has to say about the end of this present life.

In the past Christians took great comfort from the Lord's promise that he would return in glory. We can still find such comfort in this belief today. Billy Graham summarized it well: "Our world is filled with fear, hate, lust, greed, war, and utter despair. Surely the Second Coming of Jesus Christ is the only hope of replacing these depressing features with trust, love, universal peace, and prosperity."

> *I, the Son of Man, will come in the glory of my Father with his angels and will judge all people according to their deeds.*
> MATTHEW 16:27

> *If a person is ashamed of me and my message, I, the Son of Man, will be ashamed of that person when I return in my glory and in the glory of the Father and the holy angels.*
> LUKE 9:26

> *No one knows the day or the hour when these things will happen, not even the angels in heaven or the Son himself. Only the Father knows.*
> *When the Son of Man returns, it will be like it was in Noah's day. In those days before the Flood, the people were enjoying banquets and parties and weddings right up to the time Noah entered his boat. People didn't realize what was going to happen until the Flood came and swept them all away. That is the way it will be when the Son of Man comes.*

Two men will be working together in the field; one will be taken, the other left. Two women will be grinding flour at the mill; one will be taken, the other left. So be prepared, because you don't know what day your Lord is coming.

MATTHEW 24:36-42

In the Gospels Jesus promises his return but names no specific time. The promise is intended to give people hope, but Jesus makes it clear that it should do more than that. It should cause us to live in such a way that constantly reflects our readiness to meet our Lord.

The coming of the Son of Man can be compared with that of a man who left home to go on a trip. He gave each of his employees instructions about the work they were to do, and he told the gatekeeper to watch for his return. So keep a sharp lookout! For you do not know when the homeowner will return—at evening, midnight, early dawn, or late daybreak. Don't let him find you sleeping when he arrives without warning.

MARK 13:34-36

Watch out! Don't let me find you living in careless ease and drunkenness, and filled with the worries of this life. Don't let that day catch you unaware, as in a trap. For that day will come upon everyone living on the earth. Keep a constant watch. And pray that, if possible, you may escape these horrors and stand before the Son of Man.

LUKE 21:34-36

I can tell you this directly from the Lord: We who are still living when the Lord returns will not rise to meet him ahead of those who are in their graves. For the Lord himself will come down from heaven with a commanding shout, with the call of the archangel, and with the trumpet call of God. First, all the Christians who have died will rise from their graves. Then, together with them, we who are still alive and remain on the earth will be caught up in the clouds to meet the Lord in the air and remain with him forever. So comfort and encourage each other with these words.

1 THESSALONIANS 4:15-18

You know quite well that the day of the Lord will come unexpectedly, like a thief in the night. When people are saying, "All is well; everything is peaceful and secure," then disaster will fall upon them as suddenly as a woman's birth pains begin when her child is about to be born. And there will be no escape.

1 THESSALONIANS 5:2-3

The Bible ends, appropriately, with both a prayer and a promise: Jesus is coming.

"See, I am coming soon, and my reward is with me, to repay all according to their deeds."

He who is the faithful witness to all these things says, "Yes, I am coming soon!"

Amen! Come, Lord Jesus!

REVELATION 22:12, 20

See also Eternal Life, Heaven, Hell.

Joy

Christian author C. S. Lewis titled his autobiography *Surprised by Joy*. He believed that joy was a key part of the Christian life, one too often neglected.

Christianity has a reputation for being the "don't" religion—a killjoy faith designed to keep people from enjoying their lives. Nothing could be more untrue. The Old and New Testaments promise us joy—not a temporary, fleeting "high" but something that endures through both good and bad times.

> *This is the day the LORD has made. We will rejoice and be glad in it.*
>
> PSALM 118:24

> *His anger lasts for a moment, but his favor lasts a lifetime! Weeping may go on all night, but joy comes with the morning.*
>
> *You have turned my mourning into joyful dancing. You have taken away my clothes of mourning and clothed me with joy.*
>
> PSALM 30:5, 11

> *In him our hearts rejoice, for we are trusting in his holy name.*
>
> PSALM 33:21

> *The godly will rejoice in the LORD and find shelter in him. And those who do what is right will praise him.*
>
> PSALM 64:10

Let the godly rejoice. Let them be glad in God's presence. Let them be filled with joy.

PSALM 68:3

Happy are those who hear the joyful call to worship, for they will walk in the light of your presence, LORD. They rejoice all day long in your wonderful reputation. They exult in your righteousness.

PSALM 89:15-16

Light shines on the godly, and joy on those who do right. May all who are godly be happy in the LORD and praise his holy name!

PSALM 97:11-12

I have loved you even as the Father has loved me. Remain in my love. When you obey me, you remain in my love, just as I obey my Father and remain in his love. I have told you this so that you will be filled with my joy. Yes, your joy will overflow!

JOHN 15:9-11

The Kingdom of God is not a matter of what we eat or drink, but of living a life of goodness and peace and joy in the Holy Spirit. If you serve Christ with this attitude, you will please God. And other people will approve of you, too.

ROMANS 14:17-18

Always be full of joy in the Lord. I say it again—rejoice! Let everyone see that you are considerate in all you do. Remember, the Lord is coming soon.

Don't worry about anything; instead, pray about everything. Tell God what you need, and thank him for all he has done. If you do this, you will experience God's peace, which is far more wonderful than the human mind can understand. His peace will guard your hearts and minds as you live in Christ Jesus.

PHILIPPIANS 4:4-7

Because of our faith, Christ has brought us into this place of highest privilege where we now stand, and we confidently and joyfully look forward to sharing God's glory.

We can rejoice, too, when we run into problems and trials, for we know that they are good for us—they help us learn to endure. And endurance develops strength of character in us, and character strengthens our confident expectation of salvation.

ROMANS 5:2-4

See also Eternal Life, Faith, Hope, Worry and Anxiety.

Judging Others

Is there anything more amusing than discussing someone else's faults? This shouldn't be so, especially for Christians, but it seems to be widely regarded as an acceptable form of entertainment. Is it any surprise that most TV sitcoms are built around people tearing others down, either behind their backs or right to their faces? It's terribly funny on TV, not at all funny in real life—especially if you are the person being degraded.

The Bible has a lot to say about being judgmental. Jesus and the apostles understood clearly the human tendency to put others down. Among Christians, this even takes the form of questioning another's spiritual condition.

> The LORD doesn't make decisions the way you do! People judge by outward appearance, but the LORD looks at a person's thoughts and intentions.
>
> 1 SAMUEL 16:7

> Stop judging others, and you will not be judged. For others will treat you as you treat them. Whatever measure you use in judging others, it will be used to measure how you are judged. And why worry about a speck in your friend's eye when you have a log in your own? How can you think of saying, "Let me help you get rid of that speck in your eye," when you can't see past the log in your own eye? Hypocrite! First get rid of the log from your own eye; then perhaps you will see well enough to deal with the speck in your friend's eye.
>
> MATTHEW 7:1-5

We have stopped evaluating others by what the world thinks
about them. Once I mistakenly thought of Christ that way,
as though he were merely a human being. How differently I
think about him now! What this means is that those who
become Christians become new persons. They are not the
same anymore, for the old life is gone. A new life has begun!

2 CORINTHIANS 5:16-17

Don't grumble about each other, my brothers and sisters, or
God will judge you. For look! The great Judge is coming. He
is standing at the door!

JAMES 5:9

Don't speak evil against each other, my dear brothers and
sisters. If you criticize each other and condemn each other,
then you are criticizing and condemning God's law. But you
are not a judge who can decide whether the law is right or
wrong. Your job is to obey it. God alone, who made the law,
can rightly judge among us. He alone has the power to save
or to destroy. So what right do you have to condemn your
neighbor?

JAMES 4:11-12

Whenever you speak, or whatever you do, remember that
you will be judged by the law of love, the law that set you
free. For there will be no mercy for you if you have not been
merciful to others. But if you have been merciful, then God's
mercy toward you will win out over his judgment against
you.

JAMES 2:12-13

See also Anger, Hate, Hypocrisy, The Tongue.

Loneliness

One TV talk-show host claims that loneliness is *the* great problem in our society—not poverty, not homelessness, not drugs, not crime, but just plain loneliness, that achy feeling of not being connected closely to someone. For the lonely person, the Bible promises the deepest and richest kind of fellowship—fellowship with God.

> *Turn to me and have mercy on me, for I am alone and in deep distress.*
>
> *May integrity and honesty protect me, for I put my hope in you.*
>
> PSALM 25:16, 21

> *As for me, I am poor and needy, but the Lord is thinking about me right now. You are my helper and my savior. Do not delay, O my God.*
>
> PSALM 40:17

> *Sing praises to God and to his name! Sing loud praises to him who rides the clouds. His name is the LORD—rejoice in his presence!*
>
> *Father to the fatherless, defender of widows—this is God, whose dwelling is holy. God places the lonely in families; he sets the prisoners free and gives them joy.*
>
> PSALM 68:4-6

> *I will be your Father, and you will be my sons and daughters, says the Lord Almighty.*
>
> 2 CORINTHIANS 6:18

See also Fellowship with God, Friends.

Loving God

Christian author C. S. Lewis said that "a man's spiritual health is exactly proportional to his love for God." It's true that God is concerned about our morals and about our conduct. But he is mostly concerned with our heart. Are we devoted to him? If we love other things—our family, our spouse, our friends—do we still love God *more?* If not, then, as Lewis noted, we may not be spiritually healthy.

> *Take delight in the LORD, and he will give you your heart's desires.*
>
> PSALM 37:4

> *I love all who love me. Those who search for me will surely find me.*
>
> PROVERBS 8:17

> *The LORD is close to all who call on him, yes, to all who call on him sincerely. He fulfills the desires of those who fear him; he hears their cries for help and rescues them. The LORD protects all those who love him, but he destroys the wicked.*
>
> PSALM 145:18-20

> *If you love me, obey my commandments. And I will ask the Father, and he will give you another Counselor, who will never leave you. Those who obey my commandments are the ones who love me. And because they love me, my Father will love them, and I will love them. And I will reveal myself to each one of them.*
>
> *All those who love me will do what I say. My Father will*

love them, and we will come to them and live with them. Anyone who doesn't love me will not do what I say. And remember, my words are not my own. This message is from the Father who sent me.

JOHN 14:15-16, 21, 23-24

No eye has seen, no ear has heard, and no mind has imagined what God has prepared for those who love him.

1 CORINTHIANS 2:9

One day an expert in religious law stood up to test Jesus by asking him this question: "Teacher, what must I do to receive eternal life?"

Jesus replied, "What does the law of Moses say? How do you read it?"

The man answered, " 'You must love the Lord your God with all your heart, all your soul, all your strength, and all your mind.' And, 'Love your neighbor as yourself.' "

"Right!" Jesus told him. "Do this and you will live!"

LUKE 10:25-28

If someone says, "I love God," but hates a Christian brother or sister, that person is a liar; for if we don't love people we can see, how can we love God, whom we have not seen? And God himself has commanded that we must love not only him but our Christian brothers and sisters, too.

1 JOHN 4:20-21

See also Fellowship with God.

Loving Others

Loving other people doesn't mean being "in love" with everyone. "Warm-fuzzy" love is easy—until the emotion starts to fade, that is. But the human love the Bible talks about isn't just a passing emotional state. It's something based on *choice*. We *choose* to care about another person's welfare, even if that person has hurt us, called us names, ignored us. Parents understand this kind of love, for they keep loving their children even when the children don't seem to love them back. A parent's love is similar—but not as steadfast—as God's love for us. God loves us when we aren't at all lovable, and he gives us this command: "Love other people the way I love you. Make *giving*, not *getting*, the goal of your love."

> *Hatred stirs up quarrels, but love covers all offenses.*
>
> PROVERBS 10:12

> *A friend is always loyal, and a brother is born to help in time of need.*
>
> PROVERBS 17:17

> *Do for others as you would like them to do for you.*
>
> *Do you think you deserve credit merely for loving those who love you? Even the sinners do that! And if you do good only to those who do good to you, is that so wonderful? Even sinners do that much! And if you lend money only to those who can repay you, what good is that? Even sinners will lend to their own kind for a full return.*
>
> *Love your enemies! Do good to them! Lend to them! And don't be concerned that they might not repay. Then your*

reward from heaven will be very great, and you will truly be acting as children of the Most High, for he is kind to the unthankful and to those who are wicked. You must be compassionate, just as your Father is compassionate.

LUKE 6:31-36

One day an expert in religious law stood up to test Jesus by asking him this question: "Teacher, what must I do to receive eternal life?"

Jesus replied, "What does the law of Moses say? How do you read it?"

The man answered, "'You must love the Lord your God with all your heart, all your soul, all your strength, and all your mind.' And, 'Love your neighbor as yourself.'"

"Right!" Jesus told him. "Do this and you will live!"

LUKE 10:25-28

Pay all your debts, except the debt of love for others. You can never finish paying that! If you love your neighbor, you will fulfill all the requirements of God's law. For the commandments against adultery and murder and stealing and coveting—and any other commandment—are all summed up in this one commandment: "Love your neighbor as yourself." Love does no wrong to anyone, so love satisfies all of God's requirements.

ROMANS 13:8-10

If I could speak in any language in heaven or on earth but didn't love others, I would only be making meaningless noise like a loud gong or a clanging cymbal. If I had the gift of prophecy, and if I knew all the mysteries of the future and knew everything about everything, but didn't love others, what good would I be? And if I had the gift of faith so that I could speak to a mountain and make it move, without love I would be no good to anybody. If I gave everything I have to the poor and even sacrificed my body, I could boast about it;

but if I didn't love others, I would be of no value whatsoever.

Love is patient and kind. Love is not jealous or boastful or
proud or rude. Love does not demand its own way. Love is
not irritable, and it keeps no record of when it has been
wronged. It is never glad about injustice but rejoices whenever
the truth wins out. Love never gives up, never loses faith, is
always hopeful, and endures through every circumstance.

Love will last forever, but prophecy and speaking in tongues
and special knowledge will all disappear. For even our special
knowledge is incomplete, and our prophecy is incomplete. But
when the end comes, these special gifts will all disappear.

It's like this: When I was a child, I spoke and thought and
reasoned as a child does. But when I grew up, I put away
childish things. Now we see things imperfectly as in a poor
mirror, but then we will see everything with perfect clarity. All
that I know now is partial and incomplete, but then I will
know everything completely, just as God knows me now.

There are three things that will endure—faith, hope, and
love—and the greatest of these is love.

1 CORINTHIANS 13:1-13

Everyone who believes that Jesus is the Christ is a child of
God. And everyone who loves the Father loves his children,
too. We know we love God's children if we love God and
obey his commandments.

1 JOHN 5:1-2

See also Forgiving Others, Mercy.

Lying

A stand-up comic told his audience, "I wanted to go into politics, but I had this bad habit of telling the truth." Dishonesty has become so commonplace in politics, in business, and in the world in general that it seems downright normal. But people *know* instinctively that they should tell the truth. We certainly expect it from others, knowing that the world can't function if no one is trustworthy. The Bible takes lying so seriously that one of the Ten Commandments forbids it: "Do not testify falsely against your neighbor" (Exodus 20:16).

> *The LORD hates cheating, but he delights in honesty.*
>
> PROVERBS 11:1

> *Truth stands the test of time; lies are soon exposed.*
>
> PROVERBS 12:19

> *Telling lies about others is as harmful as hitting them with an ax, wounding them with a sword, or shooting them with a sharp arrow.*
>
> PROVERBS 25:18

> *Though everyone else in the world is a liar, God is true.*
>
> ROMANS 3:4

> *Do not testify spitefully against innocent neighbors; don't lie about them. And don't say, "Now I can pay them back for all their meanness to me! I'll get even!"*
>
> PROVERBS 24:28-29

People with integrity have firm footing, but those who follow crooked paths will slip and fall.

The godly person gives wise advice, but the tongue that deceives will be cut off.

PROVERBS 10:9, 31

Don't lie to each other, for you have stripped off your old evil nature and all its wicked deeds.

COLOSSIANS 3:9

See also The Tongue.

Marriage

The wisecracking Mae West was quoted as saying, "Marriage is a great institution, but I'm not ready for an institution." Sometimes it appears that most people share Mae's cynical view of marriage. Divorce is so common that hardly anyone thinks of it as a tragedy anymore—except, perhaps, the ones experiencing it. Somewhere along the line the idea of *permanence* was thrown aside. "Till death do us part" is still part of most wedding ceremonies, but we wonder if the two people take the words seriously.

The Bible has a high view of marriage. It is to be a lifetime plan, not something that can be disposed of in a lawyer's office. The love of husband and wife is, at its best, a hint of the deeper love between Christ and the church.

> *Give honor to marriage, and remain faithful to one another in marriage. God will surely judge people who are immoral and those who commit adultery.*
>
> HEBREWS 13:4

> *Drink water from your own well—share your love only with your wife. Why spill the water of your springs in public, having sex with just anyone? You should reserve it for yourselves. Don't share it with strangers.*
>
> *Let your wife be a fountain of blessing for you. Rejoice in the wife of your youth. . . . May you always be captivated by her love.*
>
> PROVERBS 5:15-19

> *The man who finds a wife finds a treasure and receives favor from the LORD.*
>
> PROVERBS 18:22

The apostle Paul, who was single, recommended the single life for people like himself who are dedicated to God's service. But Paul was realistic enough to know that many people, no matter how deep their faith, are better off married than facing the temptations of the single life.

> Because there is so much sexual immorality, each man should have his own wife, and each woman should have her own husband.
>
> The husband should not deprive his wife of sexual intimacy, which is her right as a married woman, nor should the wife deprive her husband. I wish everyone could get along without marrying, just as I do. But we are not all the same. God gives some the gift of marriage, and to others he gives the gift of singleness.
>
> Now I say to those who aren't married and to widows—it's better to stay unmarried, just as I am. But if they can't control themselves, they should go ahead and marry. It's better to marry than to burn with lust.
>
> 1 CORINTHIANS 7:2-3, 7-9

Paul also addressed a ticklish situation: What if a Christian's spouse is not a Christian?

> Now, I will speak to the rest of you, though I do not have a direct command from the Lord. If a Christian man has a wife who is an unbeliever and she is willing to continue living with him, he must not leave her. And if a Christian woman has a husband who is an unbeliever, and he is willing to continue living with her, she must not leave him. For the Christian wife brings holiness to her marriage, and the Christian husband brings holiness to his marriage. Otherwise, your children would not have a godly influence, but now they are set apart for him. (But if the husband or wife who isn't a Christian insists on leaving, let them go. In such cases the Christian husband or wife is not required to stay with them,

*for God wants his children to live in peace.) You wives must
remember that your husbands might be converted because of
you. And you husbands must remember that your wives
might be converted because of you.*

1 CORINTHIANS 7:12-16

Paul had much to say on the subject of marriage. He has
been accused of being antiwoman because of his discus-
sion of a wife's submission. The passage here will show
that he did *not* have in mind an abusive or dominating relationship but one based on mutual love.

*You will submit to one another out of reverence for Christ.
You wives will submit to your husbands as you do to the
Lord. For a husband is the head of his wife as Christ is the
head of his body, the church; he gave his life to be her Savior.
As the church submits to Christ, so you wives must submit
to your husbands in everything.*

*And you husbands must love your wives with the same love
Christ showed the church. He gave up his life for her to make
her holy and clean, washed by baptism and God's word. He
did this to present her to himself as a glorious church without a
spot or wrinkle or any other blemish. Instead, she will be holy
and without fault. In the same way, husbands ought to love
their wives as they love their own bodies. For a man is actually
loving himself when he loves his wife. No one hates his own
body but lovingly cares for it, just as Christ cares for his body,
which is the church. And we are his body.*

*As the Scriptures say, "A man leaves his father and mother
and is joined to his wife, and the two are united into one." This
is a great mystery, but it is an illustration of the way Christ and
the church are one. So again I say, each man must love his wife
as he loves himself, and the wife must respect her husband.*

EPHESIANS 5:21-33

See also Adultery, Children, Parents.

Mercy

"Mercy's indeed the attribute of heaven," wrote an English poet. The Bible indicates that not only does God show mercy to people, but people can—*must*—show mercy to each other. Grudges and getting even are a normal part of the world scene, but they have no place in the life of someone who has enjoyed the mercy of God.

The Bible promises blessing for people who can mirror God's mercy. It promises something else for those who refuse.

> *God blesses those who are merciful, for they will be shown mercy.*
>
> MATTHEW 5:7

> *There will be no mercy for you if you have not been merciful to others. But if you have been merciful, then God's mercy toward you will win out over his judgment against you.*
>
> JAMES 2:13

> *Since God chose you to be the holy people whom he loves, you must clothe yourselves with tenderhearted mercy, kindness, humility, gentleness, and patience. You must make allowance for each other's faults and forgive the person who offends you. Remember, the Lord forgave you, so you must forgive others. And the most important piece of clothing you must wear is love. Love is what binds us all together in perfect harmony. And let the peace that comes from Christ rule in your hearts. For as members of one body you are all called to live in peace. And always be thankful.*
>
> COLOSSIANS 3:12-15

Don't repay evil for evil. Don't retaliate when people say unkind things about you. Instead, pay them back with a blessing. That is what God wants you to do, and he will bless you for it.

1 PETER 3:9

Love your enemies! Do good to them! Lend to them! And don't be concerned that they might not repay. Then your reward from heaven will be very great, and you will truly be acting as children of the Most High, for he is kind to the unthankful and to those who are wicked. You must be compassionate, just as your Father is compassionate.

Stop judging others, and you will not be judged. Stop criticizing others, or it will all come back on you. If you forgive others, you will be forgiven. If you give, you will receive.

LUKE 6:35-38

One great illustration of mercy is Jesus' parable of the Good Samaritan.

He asked Jesus, "And who is my neighbor?"

Jesus replied with an illustration: "A Jewish man was traveling on a trip from Jerusalem to Jericho, and he was attacked by bandits. They stripped him of his clothes and money, beat him up, and left him half dead beside the road.

"By chance a Jewish priest came along; but when he saw the man lying there, he crossed to the other side of the road and passed him by. A Temple assistant walked over and looked at him lying there, but he also passed by on the other side.

"Then a despised Samaritan came along, and when he saw the man, he felt deep pity. Kneeling beside him, the Samaritan soothed his wounds with medicine and bandaged them. Then he put the man on his own donkey and took him to an inn, where he took care of him. The next day he handed the innkeeper two pieces of silver and told him to take care of the

man. 'If his bill runs higher than that,' he said, 'I'll pay the difference the next time I am here.'

"Now which of these three would you say was a neighbor to the man who was attacked by bandits?" Jesus asked.

The man replied, "The one who showed him mercy."

Then Jesus said, "Yes, now go and do the same."

LUKE 10:29-37

See also Enemies, Forgiving Others, God's Mercy.

Money

The Bible is a spiritual book, but not so spiritual that money doesn't matter. It *does* matter, mostly because of the human inclination to worship money instead of God. It matters because from the beginning of time, human relations have been soured by greed. The popular notion "greed is good" reflects the world's wisdom, not the Word of God.

In fact, the Bible takes a position that will shock no one: Money doesn't satisfy.

> *The rich and the poor have this in common: The LORD made them both.*
>
> PROVERBS 22:2

> *Riches won't help on the day of judgment, but right living is a safeguard against death.*
> *Trust in your money and down you go! But the godly flourish like leaves in spring.*
>
> PROVERBS 11:4, 28

> *It is better to have little with fear for the LORD than to have great treasure with turmoil.*
>
> PROVERBS 15:16

> *Those who mock the poor insult their Maker; those who rejoice at the misfortune of others will be punished.*
>
> PROVERBS 17:5

> *The hot sun rises and dries up the grass; the flower withers, and its beauty fades away. So also, wealthy people will fade away with all of their achievements.*
>
> JAMES 1:11

Those who love money will never have enough. How absurd to think that wealth brings true happiness! The more you have, the more people come to help you spend it. So what is the advantage of wealth—except perhaps to watch it run through your fingers!

People who work hard sleep well, whether they eat little or much. But the rich are always worrying and seldom get a good night's sleep.

There is another serious problem I have seen in the world. Riches are sometimes hoarded to the harm of the saver, or they are put into risky investments that turn sour, and everything is lost. In the end, there is nothing left to pass on to one's children. People who live only for wealth come to the end of their lives as naked and empty-handed as on the day they were born.

And this, too, is a very serious problem. As people come into this world, so they depart. All their hard work is for nothing. They have been working for the wind, and everything will be swept away.

ECCLESIASTES 5:10-16

A person who gets ahead by oppressing the poor or by showering gifts on the rich will end in poverty.

PROVERBS 22:16

Look here, you rich people, weep and groan with anguish because of all the terrible troubles ahead of you. Your wealth is rotting away, and your fine clothes are moth-eaten rags. Your gold and silver have become worthless. The very wealth you were counting on will eat away your flesh in hell. This treasure you have accumulated will stand as evidence against you on the day of judgment. For listen! Hear the cries of the field workers whom you have cheated of their pay. The wages you held back cry out against you. The cries of the reapers have reached the ears of the Lord Almighty.

You have spent your years on earth in luxury, satisfying
your every whim. Now your hearts are nice and fat, ready for
the slaughter. You have condemned and killed good people who
had no power to defend themselves against you.

JAMES 5:1-6

Jesus, who apparently owned very little, understood that
the key problem with money is when we let it separate us
from God. It isn't bad in itself, but it is when it becomes an
idol.

No one can serve two masters. For you will hate one and
love the other, or be devoted to one and despise the other.
You cannot serve both God and money.

MATTHEW 6:24

Jesus said again, "Dear children, it is very hard to get into
the Kingdom of God. It is easier for a camel to go through
the eye of a needle than for a rich person to enter the King-
dom of God!"

The disciples were astounded. "Then who in the world can
be saved?" they asked.

Jesus looked at them intently and said, "Humanly speaking,
it is impossible. But not with God. Everything is possible with
God."

MARK 10:24-27

Paul and the other apostles knew that Christians, like
human beings in general, forget that their money should
be used to benefit others. It seems that the more we have,
the more likely we are to neglect other people and to
neglect God.

The love of money is at the root of all kinds of evil. And some people, craving money, have wandered from the faith and pierced themselves with many sorrows.

Tell those who are rich in this world not to be proud and not to trust in their money, which will soon be gone. But their trust should be in the living God, who richly gives us all we need for our enjoyment. Tell them to use their money to do good. They should be rich in good works and should give generously to those in need, always being ready to share with others whatever God has given them. By doing this they will be storing up their treasure as a good foundation for the future so that they may take hold of real life.

1 TIMOTHY 6:10, 17-19

See also Success, Worry and Anxiety.

New Birth/New Life

The words *born again* have been repeated so often that we forget their meaning. When Jesus first told Nicodemus (a very wise and religious man, by the way) that he had to be "born again," he was misunderstood. The words still are misunderstood, but there's no reason why they should be. What they mean is that the heart—the inward person, not the outward—is made new. For the person who experiences this, it is the first day of his or her new life. The body is not new, but the inner person is. The slate is wiped clean, and God views the person as brand-new. This is only the first step, of course. The newborn must grow, and some grow faster and healthier than others. But before there is growth, there must be this new birth.

> A Jewish religious leader named Nicodemus, a Pharisee, came to speak with Jesus. "Teacher," he said, "we all know that God has sent you to teach us. Your miraculous signs are proof enough that God is with you."
>
> Jesus replied, "I assure you, unless you are born again, you can never see the Kingdom of God."
>
> "What do you mean?" exclaimed Nicodemus. "How can an old man go back into his mother's womb and be born again?"
>
> Jesus replied, "The truth is, no one can enter the Kingdom of God without being born of water and the Spirit. Humans can reproduce only human life, but the Holy Spirit gives new life from heaven. So don't be surprised at my statement that you must be born again. Just as you can hear the wind but

*can't tell where it comes from or where it is going, so you can't
explain how people are born of the Spirit."*

JOHN 3:1-8

*Jesus called a small child over to him and put the child among
them. Then he said, "I assure you, unless you turn from
your sins and become as little children, you will never get
into the Kingdom of Heaven. Therefore, anyone who
becomes as humble as this little child is the greatest in the
Kingdom of Heaven."*

MATTHEW 18:2-4

*I assure you, those who listen to my message and believe in
God who sent me have eternal life. They will never be condemned for their sins, but they have already passed from
death into life.*

JOHN 5:24

*We died and were buried with Christ by baptism. And just
as Christ was raised from the dead by the glorious power of
the Father, now we also may live new lives.*

*Since we have been united with him in his death, we will
also be raised as he was. Our old sinful selves were crucified
with Christ so that sin might lose its power in our lives. We are
no longer slaves to sin. For when we died with Christ we were
set free from the power of sin. And since we died with Christ,
we know we will also share his new life.*

ROMANS 6:4-8

*Those who become Christians become new persons. They
are not the same anymore, for the old life is gone. A new life
has begun!*

2 CORINTHIANS 5:17

It is by his boundless mercy that God has given us the privilege of being born again. Now we live with a wonderful expectation because Jesus Christ rose again from the dead.

For you have been born again. Your new life did not come from your earthly parents because the life they gave you will end in death. But this new life will last forever because it comes from the eternal, living word of God.

1 PETER 1:3, 23

Can a person lie or be deceived about being born again? Certainly. Jesus and the apostles understood this. While they warned against judging other people's spiritual condition, they did promise that we could know from a person's "fruit" whether there had really been a new birth.

If we love our Christian brothers and sisters, it proves that we have passed from death to eternal life. But a person who has no love is still dead.

1 JOHN 3:14

A healthy tree produces good fruit, and an unhealthy tree produces bad fruit. A good tree can't produce bad fruit, and a bad tree can't produce good fruit. So every tree that does not produce good fruit is chopped down and thrown into the fire. Yes, the way to identify a tree or a person is by the kind of fruit that is produced.

Not all people who sound religious are really godly. They may refer to me as "Lord," but they still won't enter the Kingdom of Heaven. The decisive issue is whether they obey my Father in heaven.

MATTHEW 7:17-21

Prove by the way you live that you have really turned from your sins and turned to God.

MATTHEW 3:8

See also Baptism of the Spirit/Gifts of the Spirit, Repentance, Salvation.

Parents

What purpose do parents serve in the modern world? Sometimes parents feel like unpaid chauffeurs, driving their children to and from ball games, band practice, whatever. With families on the move, each member pursuing his own individual plans, and precious little time for family togetherness, parents may wonder if they're really necessary for their children. Surrounded by educational and psychological "experts" on child rearing, too many parents feel inadequate for the task. Odd, since parents have been raising their children for centuries and usually have been pretty successful at it.

The Bible gives parents a much more important role than chauffeurs. In fact, parents are so important that one of the Ten Commandments concerns them:

> *Honor your father and mother. Then you will live a long, full life in the land the LORD your God will give you.*
>
> EXODUS 20:12

Going against the grain of the world, the Bible imposes an important role on parents: discipline. It is an unpopular word these days. When have you seen a TV sitcom family that had a sane view of discipline? But parental discipline is a reflection of God himself.

> *The LORD is like a father to his children, tender and compassionate to those who fear him. For he understands how weak we are; he knows we are only dust.*
>
> PSALM 103:13-14

The LORD corrects those he loves, just as a father corrects a child in whom he delights.

PROVERBS 3:12

Teach your children to choose the right path, and when they are older, they will remain upon it.

PROVERBS 22:6

Don't fail to correct your children. They won't die if you spank them. Physical discipline may well save them from death.

PROVERBS 23:13-14

Does this sound harsh? It shouldn't—nothing in the Bible condones child abuse. In fact, Christian parents are often reminded to temper discipline with kindness.

Now a word to you fathers. Don't make your children angry by the way you treat them. Rather, bring them up with the discipline and instruction approved by the Lord.

EPHESIANS 6:4

In both the Old and New Testaments, people of faith are given a critical role: passing on the heritage of faith to their children.

We will not hide these truths from our children but will tell the next generation about the glorious deeds of the LORD. We will tell of his power and the mighty miracles he did. For he issued his decree to Jacob; he gave his law to Israel. He commanded our ancestors to teach them to their children, so the next generation might know them—even the children not yet born—that they in turn might teach their children. So each generation can set its hope anew on God, remembering his glorious miracles and obeying his commands. Then they will not be like their ancestors—stubborn, rebellious, and unfaithful, refusing to give their hearts to God.

PSALM 78:4-8

See also Children, Marriage.

Patience

You may have seen the popular wall poster of a few years ago with the words *Give me patience, and I want it right NOW!* Patience seems to be in small supply in our instant gratification world. Yet for people who continually describe themselves as stressed-out, it might be the most useful quality we could hope for.

> Be still in the presence of the LORD, and wait patiently for him to act. Don't worry about evil people who prosper or fret about their wicked schemes.
>
> Stop your anger! Turn from your rage! Do not envy others—it only leads to harm. For the wicked will be destroyed, but those who trust in the LORD will possess the land.
>
> PSALM 37:7-9

> It is better to be patient than powerful; it is better to have self-control than to conquer a city.
>
> PROVERBS 16:32

> Patience can persuade a prince, and soft speech can crush strong opposition.
>
> PROVERBS 25:15

> Patience is better than pride.
>
> Don't be quick-tempered, for anger is the friend of fools.
>
> ECCLESIASTES 7:8-9

Love is patient and kind. Love is not jealous or boastful or proud or rude. Love does not demand its own way. Love is not irritable, and it keeps no record of when it has been wronged.

1 CORINTHIANS 13:4-5

We can rejoice, too, when we run into problems and trials, for we know that they are good for us—they help us learn to endure. And endurance develops strength of character in us, and character strengthens our confident expectation of salvation.

ROMANS 5:3-4

We also pray that you will be strengthened with his glorious power so that you will have all the patience and endurance you need. May you be filled with joy, always thanking the Father, who has enabled you to share the inheritance that belongs to God's holy people, who live in the light.

COLOSSIANS 1:11-12

Do not throw away this confident trust in the Lord, no matter what happens. Remember the great reward it brings you! Patient endurance is what you need now, so you will continue to do God's will. Then you will receive all that he has promised.

For in just a little while, the Coming One will come and not delay. And a righteous person will live by faith. But I will have no pleasure in anyone who turns away.

HEBREWS 10:35-38

Dear brothers and sisters, whenever trouble comes your way, let it be an opportunity for joy. For when your faith is tested, your endurance has a chance to grow. So let it grow, for when your endurance is fully developed, you will be strong in character and ready for anything.

JAMES 1:2-4

If you suffer for doing right and are patient beneath the blows, God is pleased with you.

This suffering is all part of what God has called you to. Christ, who suffered for you, is your example. Follow in his steps.

1 PETER 2:20-21

Jesus said, "Come to me, all of you who are weary and carry heavy burdens, and I will give you rest. Take my yoke upon you. Let me teach you, because I am humble and gentle, and you will find rest for your souls. For my yoke fits perfectly, and the burden I give you is light."

MATTHEW 11:28-30

See also Worry and Anxiety.

Peace

It is curious that with all our timesaving and laborsaving devices (things our ancestors might have yearned for), we still seem incredibly rushed, hassled, often perceiving life as a struggle with no end in sight. No wonder peace sounds so attractive to us.

Turn on the nightly news, and you'll notice that the politicians of the world haven't done well at bringing peace. Nor is this likely to happen. It is useless to wait for governments to bring peace. Anyway, peace doesn't just mean the absence of war. It means harmony within individuals and between people. This kind of peace can be had in the midst of our own hectic, stress-filled life.

> You will keep in perfect peace all who trust in you, whose thoughts are fixed on you!
>
> ISAIAH 26:3

> "There is no peace for the wicked," says the LORD.
>
> ISAIAH 48:22

> God blesses those who work for peace, for they will be called the children of God.
>
> MATTHEW 5:9

> I will lie down in peace and sleep, for you alone, O LORD, will keep me safe.
>
> PSALM 4:8

I listen carefully to what God the LORD is saying, for he speaks peace to his people, his faithful ones.

PSALM 85:8

When the ways of people please the LORD, he makes even their enemies live at peace with them.

PROVERBS 16:7

A dry crust eaten in peace is better than a great feast with strife.

PROVERBS 17:1

If your sinful nature controls your mind, there is death. But if the Holy Spirit controls your mind, there is life and peace.

ROMANS 8:6

Since we have been made right in God's sight by faith, we have peace with God because of what Jesus Christ our Lord has done for us.

ROMANS 5:1

I pray that God, who gives you hope, will keep you happy and full of peace as you believe in him. May you overflow with hope through the power of the Holy Spirit.

ROMANS 15:13

The God of peace will soon crush Satan under your feet.

ROMANS 16:20

When the Holy Spirit controls our lives, he will produce this kind of fruit in us: love, joy, peace, patience, kindness, goodness, faithfulness, gentleness, and self-control. Here there is no conflict with the law.

GALATIANS 5:22-23

The first Christians knew that one great enemy of peace is worry. We worry because we lack faith that God cares for us. So we often deprive ourselves of peace because of our lack of faith in God's continuous care. Paul assures Christians that God offers them something greater than a life of worry.

> *Don't worry about anything; instead, pray about everything. Tell God what you need, and thank him for all he has done. If you do this, you will experience God's peace, which is far more wonderful than the human mind can understand. His peace will guard your hearts and minds as you live in Christ Jesus.*
>
> *Keep putting into practice all you learned from me and heard from me and saw me doing, and the God of peace will be with you.*
>
> PHILIPPIANS 4:6-7, 9

> *Let the peace that comes from Christ rule in your hearts. For as members of one body you are all called to live in peace. And always be thankful.*
>
> COLOSSIANS 3:15

> *There will be glory and honor and peace from God for all who do good.*
>
> ROMANS 2:10

> *Try to live in peace with everyone, and seek to live a clean and holy life, for those who are not holy will not see the Lord.*
>
> HEBREWS 12:14

Jesus, who was persecuted to the point of death, knew that his followers would also face persecution. He gave them a promise: peace, even with persecution or the threat of persecution.

> *I am leaving you with a gift—peace of mind and heart. And the peace I give isn't like the peace the world gives. So don't be troubled or afraid.*
>
> JOHN 14:27

> *I have told you all this so that you may have peace in me. Here on earth you will have many trials and sorrows. But take heart, because I have overcome the world.*
>
> JOHN 16:33

See also Contentment, Trusting God, Worry and Anxiety.

Prayer

Prayer is a popular subject among religious people. Books have been written about it, and you can even attend seminars and workshops on prayer. The odd thing is that most people *do not pray regularly.*

But the Bible is brimming over with promises about prayer: Prayer brings us into God's presence. Prayer changes people. Prayer changes the world.

> *The LORD is close to all who call on him, yes, to all who call on him sincerely. He fulfills the desires of those who fear him; he hears their cries for help and rescues them.*
>
> PSALM 145:18-19

> *The eyes of the LORD watch over those who do right; his ears are open to their cries for help.*
>
> *The LORD hears his people when they call to him for help. He rescues them from all their troubles.*
>
> PSALM 34:15, 17

> *The LORD says, "I will rescue those who love me. I will protect those who trust in my name. When they call on me, I will answer; I will be with them in trouble. I will rescue them and honor them. I will satisfy them with a long life and give them my salvation."*
>
> PSALM 91:14-16

In our instant-gratification society, prayer seems out of place. We pray for something and expect it to happen immediately—or soon, anyway. The Bible promises answers, but not immediate ones. The two following passages from the Gospels depict Jesus recommending *perseverance* in prayer.

One day Jesus told his disciples a story to illustrate their need for constant prayer and to show them that they must never give up. "There was a judge in a certain city," he said, "who was a godless man with great contempt for everyone. A widow of that city came to him repeatedly, appealing for justice against someone who had harmed her. The judge ignored her for a while, but eventually she wore him out. 'I fear neither God nor man,' he said to himself, 'but this woman is driving me crazy. I'm going to see that she gets justice, because she is wearing me out with her constant requests!'"

Then the Lord said, "Learn a lesson from this evil judge. Even he rendered a just decision in the end, so don't you think God will surely give justice to his chosen people who plead with him day and night? Will he keep putting them off? I tell you, he will grant justice to them quickly! But when I, the Son of Man, return, how many will I find who have faith?"

LUKE 18:1-8

Keep on asking, and you will be given what you ask for. Keep on looking, and you will find. Keep on knocking, and the door will be opened. For everyone who asks, receives. Everyone who seeks, finds. And the door is opened to everyone who knocks. You parents—if your children ask for a loaf of bread, do you give them a stone instead? Or if they ask for a fish, do you give them a snake? Of course not! If you sinful people know how to give good gifts to your children, how much more will your heavenly Father give good gifts to those who ask him.

MATTHEW 7:7-11

> We can be confident that he will listen to us whenever we
> ask him for anything in line with his will. And if we know he
> is listening when we make our requests, we can be sure that
> he will give us what we ask for.

> 1 JOHN 5:14-15

> Don't worry about anything; instead, pray about everything.
> Tell God what you need, and thank him for all he has done.
> If you do this, you will experience God's peace, which is far
> more wonderful than the human mind can understand. His
> peace will guard your hearts and minds as you live in Christ
> Jesus.

> PHILIPPIANS 4:6-7

Jesus understood the importance of prayer. But he also
understood that some people like to make a show out of
it, trying to impress others with their long and flowery
prayers. He assured his followers that this kind of prayer
had no influence with God, who understands our motives.

> When you pray, go away by yourself, shut the door behind
> you, and pray to your Father secretly. Then your Father,
> who knows all secrets, will reward you.
> When you pray, don't babble on and on as people of other
> religions do. They think their prayers are answered only by
> repeating their words again and again. Don't be like them,
> because your Father knows exactly what you need even before
> you ask him!

> MATTHEW 6:6-8

Some people claim they don't know *how* to pray. The Bible
is full of examples, including the famous Lord's Prayer
(Matthew 6:9-13 and Luke 11:2-4). But the Bible also promises that our awkwardness at praying does not need to hold

us back. God has given us a "prayer partner," the Holy Spirit.

> *The Holy Spirit helps us in our distress. For we don't even know what we should pray for, nor how we should pray. But the Holy Spirit prays for us with groanings that cannot be expressed in words.*

ROMANS 8:26

See also Confessing Sin, Fellowship with God.

Pride and Conceit

People can take pride in practically anything—their looks, possessions, intelligence, job, sophistication, family connections, even their religion. Does God deny us the enjoyment of being attractive, of owning a home or car, of having a good education, of having some achievements in life? Of course not. None of these things are wrong in themselves. When the Bible talks about pride and arrogance, it is talking about making idols—gods—of these things. It is talking about thinking of ourselves so highly that God has no place in our life.

> *Stop acting so proud and haughty! Don't speak with such arrogance! The LORD is a God who knows your deeds; and he will judge you for what you have done.*
>
> 1 SAMUEL 2:3

> *Love the LORD, all you faithful ones! For the LORD protects those who are loyal to him, but he harshly punishes all who are arrogant.*
>
> PSALM 31:23

> *Don't be impressed with your own wisdom. Instead, fear the LORD and turn your back on evil. Then you will gain renewed health and vitality.*
>
> PROVERBS 3:7-8

The LORD despises pride; be assured that the proud will be punished.

Pride goes before destruction, and haughtiness before a fall.

It is better to live humbly with the poor than to share plunder with the proud.

PROVERBS 16:5, 18-19

Haughty eyes, a proud heart, and evil actions are all sin.
PROVERBS 21:4

The day is coming when your pride will be brought low and the LORD alone will be exalted. In that day the LORD Almighty will punish the proud, bringing them down to the dust.

ISAIAH 2:11-12

I, the LORD, will punish the world for its evil and the wicked for their sin. I will crush the arrogance of the proud and the haughtiness of the mighty.

ISAIAH 13:11

Look at the proud! They trust in themselves, and their lives are crooked; but the righteous will live by their faith.
HABAKKUK 2:4

God blesses those who realize their need for him, for the Kingdom of Heaven is given to them. God blesses those who are gentle and lowly, for the whole earth will belong to them.
MATTHEW 5:3, 5

Jesus prayed this prayer: "O Father, Lord of heaven and earth, thank you for hiding the truth from those who think themselves so wise and clever, and for revealing it to the childlike."

MATTHEW 11:25

Anyone who wants to be the first must take last place and be the servant of everyone else.

MARK 9:35

The world offers only the lust for physical pleasure, the lust for everything we see, and pride in our possessions. These are not from the Father. They are from this evil world.

1 JOHN 2:16

The worst kind of pride is spiritual pride. Jesus understood this, knowing that people who appear religious can be incredibly vain. One of his classic parables looks at this problem, promising a blessing not on the spiritually proud but on those who humble themselves before God.

Jesus told this story to some who had great self-confidence and scorned everyone else: "Two men went to the Temple to pray. One was a Pharisee, and the other was a dishonest tax collector. The proud Pharisee stood by himself and prayed this prayer: 'I thank you, God, that I am not a sinner like everyone else, especially like that tax collector over there! For I never cheat, I don't sin, I don't commit adultery, I fast twice a week, and I give you a tenth of my income.'

"But the tax collector stood at a distance and dared not even lift his eyes to heaven as he prayed. Instead, he beat his chest in sorrow, saying, 'O God, be merciful to me, for I am a sinner.' I tell you, this sinner, not the Pharisee, returned home justified before God. For the proud will be humbled, but the humble will be honored."

LUKE 18:9-14

See also Hypocrisy, Money, Success.

Repentance

The word *repentance* has gone out of style, although the word *change* is certainly popular. Change is part of repentance, of course. In fact, it is the forgotten part. We have the strange idea that repentance simply means saying to God, with tears in our eyes, "I'm sorry." Well, that is step one. Step two, more important than the tears, is change. Martin Luther put it this way: "To do so no more is the truest repentance." In other words, if we are gossiping, cheating, committing some sexual sin, or being just plain selfish, the response to God is "I'm truly sorry," followed by "I won't do it again."

The good news is, God accepts this—joyfully, in fact.

> *If my people who are called by my name will humble themselves and pray and seek my face and turn from their wicked ways, I will hear from heaven and will forgive their sins and heal their land.*
>
> 2 CHRONICLES 7:14

> *If we confess our sins to him, he is faithful and just to forgive us and to cleanse us from every wrong.*
>
> 1 JOHN 1:9

The Bible's great song of repentance is Psalm 51, written by King David himself. It expresses the desire—and the expectation—that God will forgive the believer's sin and will restore the broken relationship.

*Purify me from my sins, and I will be clean; wash me, and I
will be whiter than snow. Oh, give me back my joy again;
you have broken me—now let me rejoice. Don't keep looking at my sins. Remove the stain of my guilt. Create in me a
clean heart, O God. Renew a right spirit within me. Do not
banish me from your presence, and don't take your Holy
Spirit from me. Restore to me again the joy of your salvation, and make me willing to obey you. Then I will teach
your ways to sinners, and they will return to you.*

*You would not be pleased with sacrifices, or I would bring
them. If I brought you a burnt offering, you would not accept
it. The sacrifice you want is a broken spirit. A broken and
repentant heart, O God, you will not despise.*

PSALM 51:7-13, 16-17

People often like to think of Jesus as a great moral teacher.
He was that. But Jesus was aware that the world needed
more than just good advice and sweet sayings about love
and kindness. As the opening of Mark's Gospel makes
clear, Jesus' main message was *repentance*.

*Jesus went to Galilee to preach God's Good News. "At last
the time has come!" he announced. "The Kingdom of God is
near! Turn from your sins and believe this Good News!"*

MARK 1:14-15

*Healthy people don't need a doctor—sick people do. I have
come to call sinners to turn from their sins, not to spend my
time with those who think they are already good enough.*

LUKE 5:31-32

*The Lord isn't really being slow about his promise to return,
as some people think. No, he is being patient for your sake.
He does not want anyone to perish, so he is giving more time
for everyone to repent.*

2 PETER 3:9

One of Jesus' most famous parables is the parable of the Prodigal Son. It would be more accurate to call it the parable of the Repentant Son, or, even better, the parable of the Forgiving Father. Nowhere in the Bible are repentance and the promise of God's forgiveness made more vivid.

> A man had two sons. The younger son told his father, "I want my share of your estate now, instead of waiting until you die." So his father agreed to divide his wealth between his sons.
>
> A few days later this younger son packed all his belongings and took a trip to a distant land, and there he wasted all his money on wild living. About the time his money ran out, a great famine swept over the land, and he began to starve. He persuaded a local farmer to hire him to feed his pigs. The boy became so hungry that even the pods he was feeding the pigs looked good to him. But no one gave him anything.
>
> When he finally came to his senses, he said to himself, "At home even the hired men have food enough to spare, and here I am, dying of hunger! I will go home to my father and say, 'Father, I have sinned against both heaven and you, and I am no longer worthy of being called your son. Please take me on as a hired man.'"
>
> So he returned home to his father. And while he was still a long distance away, his father saw him coming. Filled with love and compassion, he ran to his son, embraced him, and kissed him. His son said to him, "Father, I have sinned against both heaven and you, and I am no longer worthy of being called your son."
>
> But his father said to the servants, "Quick! Bring the finest robe in the house and put it on him. Get a ring for his finger, and sandals for his feet. And kill the calf we have been fattening in the pen. We must celebrate with a feast, for this son of mine was dead and has now returned to life. He was lost, but now he is found." So the party began.

LUKE 15:11-24

See also Confessing Sin, New Birth/New Life.

Revenge

"Revenge is sweet"—in the world's view. It seems human—all *too* human—to retaliate when someone injures us. People gain pleasure sometimes from just planning revenge, even if they never carry it out. This is not only a waste of time and mental energy, but more important, it is downright wrong.

Never seek revenge or bear a grudge against anyone, but love your neighbor as yourself.

LEVITICUS 19:18

Don't say, "I will get even for this wrong." Wait for the LORD to handle the matter.

PROVERBS 20:22

If you set a trap for others, you will get caught in it yourself. If you roll a boulder down on others, it will roll back and crush you.

PROVERBS 26:27

Never pay back evil for evil to anyone. Do things in such a way that everyone can see you are honorable. Do your part to live in peace with everyone, as much as possible.

Dear friends, never avenge yourselves. Leave that to God. For it is written, "I will take vengeance; I will repay those who deserve it," says the Lord.

ROMANS 12:17-19

The classic statement on revenge is in Jesus' famous words in the Sermon on the Mount.

> You have heard that the law of Moses says, "If an eye is injured, injure the eye of the person who did it. If a tooth gets knocked out, knock out the tooth of the person who did it." But I say, don't resist an evil person! If you are slapped on the right cheek, turn the other, too. If you are ordered to court and your shirt is taken from you, give your coat, too. If a soldier demands that you carry his gear for a mile, carry it two miles. Give to those who ask, and don't turn away from those who want to borrow.
>
> You have heard that the law of Moses says, "Love your neighbor" and hate your enemy. But I say, love your enemies! Pray for those who persecute you! In that way, you will be acting as true children of your Father in heaven. For he gives his sunlight to both the evil and the good, and he sends rain on the just and on the unjust, too.

MATTHEW 5:38-45

Christians have been persecuted from the New Testament days until now. It is hard to keep from hating the persecutor. But Paul, who had endured persecution himself, told the Christians to endure it patiently, without wanting vengeance.

> God will use this persecution to show his justice. For he will make you worthy of his Kingdom, for which you are suffering, and in his justice he will punish those who persecute you. And God will provide rest for you who are being persecuted and also for us when the Lord Jesus appears from heaven. He will come with his mighty angels, in flaming fire, bringing judgment on those who don't know God and on those who refuse to obey the Good News of our Lord Jesus.

2 THESSALONIANS 1:5-8

See also Anger, Enemies, Forgiving Others, Hate.

Salvation

"Self-improvement" and "self-help" are popular concepts today, but they would have been totally meaningless to the authors of the Bible. The Bible makes no promises at all about *learning* to be a child of God or *working* to be the right kind of person. The message of salvation is that there is no *improvement*—there is *transformation*. We are changed—by God—from sinners into God's children. We are changed from being alienated from him to being reconciled to him. This isn't accomplished by reading books or attending seminars or joining a twelve-step program. It occurs by recognizing that we need *saving,* not just improving.

> *The LORD is close to the brokenhearted; he rescues those who are crushed in spirit.*
>
> PSALM 34:18

> *The LORD protects those of childlike faith; I was facing death, and then he saved me.*
>
> PSALM 116:6

Jesus came into the world, proclaiming the Kingdom of God—not a kingdom on a map, but the rule of God over those willing to be ruled by him. In other words, salvation is extended to those willing to say to God, "I don't rule my own life very well. You do it." According to Jesus, anyone can make this statement, but few do.

*You can enter God's Kingdom only through the narrow gate.
The highway to hell is broad, and its gate is wide for the
many who choose the easy way. But the gateway to life is
small, and the road is narrow, and only a few ever find it.*

MATTHEW 7:13-14

*If you try to keep your life for yourself, you will lose it. But
if you give up your life for me, you will find true life. And
how do you benefit if you gain the whole world but lose your
own soul in the process? Is anything worth more than your
soul?*

MATTHEW 16:25-26

*God so loved the world that he gave his only Son, so that
everyone who believes in him will not perish but have eternal
life. God did not send his Son into the world to condemn it,
but to save it.*

JOHN 3:16-17

*Jesus replied, "I assure you, unless you are born again, you
can never see the Kingdom of God."*

*"What do you mean?" exclaimed Nicodemus. "How can
an old man go back into his mother's womb and be born
again?"*

*Jesus replied, "The truth is, no one can enter the Kingdom
of God without being born of water and the Spirit. Humans
can reproduce only human life, but the Holy Spirit gives new
life from heaven. So don't be surprised at my statement that
you must be born again."*

JOHN 3:3-7

Paul, who wrote much of the New Testament, understood
the self-improvement mentality. He had been brought up to
believe that keeping the Jewish law was the way to please
God. He did keep it faithfully—then concluded it hadn't
made him right in God's sight. Again and again in his let-

ters, Paul reminds his readers that Christ alone is the way to salvation.

> *No one can ever be made right in God's sight by doing what his law commands. For the more we know God's law, the clearer it becomes that we aren't obeying it.*
>
> *But now God has shown us a different way of being right in his sight—not by obeying the law but by the way promised in the Scriptures long ago. We are made right in God's sight when we trust in Jesus Christ to take away our sins. And we all can be saved in this same way, no matter who we are or what we have done.*
>
> *For all have sinned; all fall short of God's glorious standard. Yet now God in his gracious kindness declares us not guilty. He has done this through Christ Jesus, who has freed us by taking away our sins.*
>
> ROMANS 3:20-24

Paul knew full well that the gospel would meet with skeptics. Do intelligent people really believe that Jesus could be the Son of God and that his being crucified could somehow make us "right in God's sight"? Actually, many intelligent people do believe this. And many don't. Paul made it clear that the message couldn't be judged just by its popularity.

> *I know very well how foolish the message of the cross sounds to those who are on the road to destruction. But we who are being saved recognize this message as the very power of God. As the Scriptures say, "I will destroy human wisdom and discard their most brilliant ideas."*
>
> 1 CORINTHIANS 1:18-19

> *Those who become Christians become new persons. They are not the same anymore, for the old life is gone. A new life has begun!*
>
> *All this newness of life is from God, who brought us back to*

himself through what Christ did. And God has given us the task of reconciling people to him. For God was in Christ, reconciling the world to himself, no longer counting people's sins against them. This is the wonderful message he has given us to tell others.

For God made Christ, who never sinned, to be the offering for our sin, so that we could be made right with God through Christ.

2 CORINTHIANS 5:17-19, 21

You were buried with Christ when you were baptized. And with him you were raised to a new life because you trusted the mighty power of God, who raised Christ from the dead.

You were dead because of your sins and because your sinful nature was not yet cut away. Then God made you alive with Christ. He forgave all our sins.

COLOSSIANS 2:12-13

He saved us, not because of the good things we did, but because of his mercy. He washed away our sins and gave us a new life through the Holy Spirit.

TITUS 3:5

I am convinced that nothing can ever separate us from his love. Death can't, and life can't. The angels can't, and the demons can't. Our fears for today, our worries about tomorrow, and even the powers of hell can't keep God's love away.

ROMANS 8:38

See also New Birth/New Life, Repentance, Sin and Redemption.

Self-Control and Self-Denial

After the 1960s, it appeared that self-control was as out-moded as the horse and buggy. Then it came back into style—in physical fitness and dieting, anyway. Sidewalks and parks across the country are cluttered with self-denying individuals beating their bodies into submission. And for what reason?

Is this the kind of self-control God desires from us? Maybe. The Bible has a few things to say about gluttony and excessive drinking. But the self-control the Bible applauds is a different thing: saying yes to God, saying no to any selfish urges that lead us away from God or hinder us from loving other people.

> *A person without self-control is as defenseless as a city with broken-down walls.*
>
> PROVERBS 25:28

> *An evil man is held captive by his own sins; they are ropes that catch and hold him. He will die for lack of self-control; he will be lost because of his incredible folly.*
>
> PROVERBS 5:22-23

> *Jesus said to the disciples, "If any of you wants to be my follower, you must put aside your selfish ambition, shoulder your cross, and follow me. If you try to keep your life for yourself, you will lose it. But if you give up your life for me, you will find true life. And how do you benefit if you gain the whole world but lose your own soul in the process? Is anything worth more than your soul? For I, the Son of Man,*

will come in the glory of my Father with his angels and will judge all people according to their deeds."

MATTHEW 16:24-27

I assure you, everyone who has given up house or wife or brothers or parents or children, for the sake of the Kingdom of God, will be repaid many times over in this life, as well as receiving eternal life in the world to come.

LUKE 18:29-30

Our old sinful selves were crucified with Christ so that sin might lose its power in our lives. We are no longer slaves to sin.

ROMANS 6:6

God has not given us a spirit of fear and timidity, but of power, love, and self-discipline.

2 TIMOTHY 1:7

When the Holy Spirit controls our lives, he will produce this kind of fruit in us: love, joy, peace, patience, kindness, goodness, faithfulness, gentleness, and self-control. Here there is no conflict with the law.

Those who belong to Christ Jesus have nailed the passions and desires of their sinful nature to his cross and crucified them there. If we are living now by the Holy Spirit, let us follow the Holy Spirit's leading in every part of our lives.

GALATIANS 5:22-25

Self-control involves more than abstaining from certain sinful behaviors. It also means resisting our natural impulse to retaliate, as Jesus made clear:

Don't resist an evil person! If you are slapped on the right cheek, turn the other, too. If you are ordered to court and your shirt is taken from you, give your coat, too. If a soldier

143

demands that you carry his gear for a mile, carry it two miles. Give to those who ask, and don't turn away from those who want to borrow.

MATTHEW 5:39-42

See also Anger, Hate, Revenge, Temptation.

Sexuality

One thing the world seems pretty certain about: Christianity is a killjoy, antisex religion. But this is a lie. Nothing in the Bible says that sex is wrong. The Bible does hold the view that sex is such a mysterious and powerful thing that it must be subject to certain boundaries—like marriage. The Bible views the body as something important—something to be taken care of and used in God's service, not used as a sexual toy.

> Put to death the sinful, earthly things lurking within you.
> Have nothing to do with sexual sin, impurity, lust, and
> shameful desires. Don't be greedy for the good things of this
> life, for that is idolatry. God's terrible anger will come upon
> those who do such things. You used to do them when your
> life was still part of this world. But now is the time to get rid
> of anger, rage, malicious behavior, slander, and dirty lan-
> guage. Don't lie to each other, for you have stripped off your
> old evil nature and all its wicked deeds. In its place you have
> clothed yourselves with a brand-new nature that is continu-
> ally being renewed as you learn more and more about
> Christ, who created this new nature within you.
>
> COLOSSIANS 3:5-10

Did you notice in the preceding passage the words *you used to do them . . .* ? This is a promise of forgiveness for people who have committed sexual sin. In the following passage from 1 Corinthians, note these important words:

There was a time when some of you were just like that.

Don't you know that those who do wrong will have no share in the Kingdom of God? Don't fool yourselves. Those who indulge in sexual sin, who are idol worshipers, adulterers, male prostitutes, homosexuals, thieves, greedy people, drunkards, abusers, and swindlers—none of these will have a share in the Kingdom of God. There was a time when some of you were just like that, but now your sins have been washed away, and you have been set apart for God. You have been made right with God because of what the Lord Jesus Christ and the Spirit of our God have done for you.

Don't you realize that your bodies are actually parts of Christ? Should a man take his body, which belongs to Christ, and join it to a prostitute? Never! And don't you know that if a man joins himself to a prostitute, he becomes one body with her? For the Scriptures say, "The two are united into one." But the person who is joined to the Lord becomes one spirit with him.

Run away from sexual sin! No other sin so clearly affects the body as this one does. For sexual immorality is a sin against your own body.

1 CORINTHIANS 6:9-11, 15-18

Give honor to marriage, and remain faithful to one another in marriage. God will surely judge people who are immoral and those who commit adultery.

HEBREWS 13:4

When you follow the desires of your sinful nature, your lives will produce these evil results: sexual immorality, impure thoughts, eagerness for lustful pleasure, idolatry, participation in demonic activities, hostility, quarreling, jealousy, outbursts of anger, selfish ambition, divisions, the feeling that everyone is wrong except those in your own little group, envy, drunkenness, wild parties, and other kinds of sin. Let me tell you again, as I have before, that anyone living that sort of life will not inherit the Kingdom of God.

GALATIANS 5:19-21

Let there be no sexual immorality, impurity, or greed among you. Such sins have no place among God's people. Obscene stories, foolish talk, and coarse jokes—these are not for you. Instead, let there be thankfulness to God. You can be sure that no immoral, impure, or greedy person will inherit the Kingdom of Christ and of God. For a greedy person is really an idolater who worships the things of this world. Don't be fooled by those who try to excuse these sins, for the terrible anger of God comes upon all those who disobey him. Don't participate in the things these people do. For though your hearts were once full of darkness, now you are full of light from the Lord, and your behavior should show it!

Take no part in the worthless deeds of evil and darkness; instead, rebuke and expose them. It is shameful even to talk about the things that ungodly people do in secret. But when the light shines on them, it becomes clear how evil these things are. . . . This is why it is said, "Awake, O sleeper, rise up from the dead, and Christ will give you light."

EPHESIANS 5:3-8, 11-14

Those who live only to satisfy their own sinful desires will harvest the consequences of decay and death. But those who live to please the Spirit will harvest everlasting life from the Spirit.

GALATIANS 6:8

See also Adultery, Self-Control and Self-Denial, Temptation.

Sickness

God cares about our spiritual life *and* our physical life. He created the human body, and he is pleased when we enjoy health and vigor. But in this world our body endures sickness, pain, and decay. Sometimes we abuse our own body, but often our ailments occur because—well, we don't always know why, nor does God promise that we will understand why.

Healing occurs—sometimes dramatically, as in the work of Jesus and his disciples. The Gospels overflow with stories of Jesus healing every kind of bodily affliction. So did his disciples, who he promised would do the same works that he did.

God still works today to heal people in ways that defy medical knowledge. It is never wrong to pray for healing, either for ourselves or others. The Bible tells us to pray for whatever we need, and that surely includes freedom from sickness and pain.

But healing does not always occur, even to the most loving, God-centered people. Why not? We don't know. But the Bible does promise us that if we are not healed in this life, there is something greater awaiting us afterward.

> O LORD, *you alone can heal me; you alone can save. My praises are for you alone!*
>
> JEREMIAH 17:14

> *I will give you back your health and heal your wounds, says the LORD.*
>
> JEREMIAH 30:17

> *Jesus called his twelve disciples to him and gave them author-*
> *ity to cast out evil spirits and to heal every kind of disease*
> *and illness.*

MATTHEW 10:1

Paul's first letter to the Corinthians tells about spiritual
gifts, one of which is healing. It is clear that the gift of healing did not end with Jesus and his disciples.

> *There are different ways God works in our lives, but it is the*
> *same God who does the work through all of us. God mani-*
> *fests the Spirit through each person for the good of the entire*
> *church.*
>
> *To one person the Spirit gives a word of special wisdom; to*
> *another he gives the gift of special knowledge. The Spirit gives*
> *special faith to another, and to someone else he gives the power*
> *to heal the sick. He gives one person the power to perform*
> *miracles, and to another the ability to prophesy. He gives*
> *someone else the ability to distinguish between spirits. Still*
> *another person is given the ability to speak in different kinds of*
> *tongues, and another is given the ability to interpret what is*
> *being said. It is the same and only Holy Spirit who distributes*
> *these gifts. He alone decides which gift each person should*
> *have.*
>
> *Now all of you together are Christ's body, and each one of*
> *you is a separate and necessary part of it. Here is a list of some*
> *of the members that God has placed in the body of Christ: first*
> *are apostles, second are prophets, third are teachers, then those*
> *who do miracles, those who have the gift of healing, those who*
> *can help others, those who can get others to work together,*
> *those who speak in different kinds of tongues.*

1 CORINTHIANS 12:6-11, 27-28

In one of Paul's letters, he talks about a "thorn in the flesh," perhaps some kind of physical ailment. Paul was certainly a man of faith, yet he was not healed. He wasn't told why. But Paul did the obvious thing in the situation: he accepted it.

> *Three different times I begged the Lord to take it away. Each time he said, "My gracious favor is all you need. My power works best in your weakness." So now I am glad to boast about my weaknesses, so that the power of Christ may work through me. Since I know it is all for Christ's good, I am quite content with my weaknesses and with insults, hardships, persecutions, and calamities. For when I am weak, then I am strong.*
>
> 2 CORINTHIANS 12:8-10

Every person who has ever been healed has died. Even Lazarus, the friend Jesus raised from the dead, died again. The Bible makes no promise that our present body, whatever its condition, will stay healthy or last forever. In fact, the Bible promises something much more glorious: a new body, like our present one but also different, a body made for eternity.

> *We know that when this earthly tent we live in is taken down—when we die and leave these bodies—we will have a home in heaven, an eternal body made for us by God himself and not by human hands. We grow weary in our present bodies, and we long for the day when we will put on our heavenly bodies like new clothing. For we will not be spirits without bodies, but we will put on new heavenly bodies. Our dying bodies make us groan and sigh, but it's not that we want to die and have no bodies at all. We want to slip into our new bodies so that these dying bodies will be swallowed up by everlasting life.*
>
> 2 CORINTHIANS 5:1-4

Though our bodies are dying, our spirits are being renewed every day.

2 CORINTHIANS 4:16

See also Comfort in Times of Trouble, Eternal Life, God's Love for Us, Patience.

Sin and Redemption

Are there any sinners around anymore? People are called "dysfunctional" or "not in touch with themselves" or "negative" or "uptight" or "immature" or even "in need of counseling"—but never "sinful." Odd that we've discarded the word *sin,* since it covers all these categories and more. It also covers all of us—not just the cruelest and most criminal but even people who seem well adjusted. The Bible assures us that we all sin. Our sin—seeking our own selfish way instead of God's way, making ourselves the center of the universe—separates us from God. It mars our relationships with others. None of this has changed, even if we throw out the word *sin* because it seems too old-fashioned.

> *The human heart is most deceitful and desperately wicked. Who really knows how bad it is? But I know! I, the LORD, search all hearts and examine secret motives. I give all people their due rewards, according to what their actions deserve.*
>
> JEREMIAH 17:9-10

> *The LORD looks down from heaven on the entire human race; he looks to see if there is even one with real understanding, one who seeks for God. But no, all have turned away from God; all have become corrupt. No one does good, not even one!*
>
> PSALM 14:2-3

God shows his anger from heaven against all sinful, wicked
people who push the truth away from themselves. For the
truth about God is known to them instinctively. God has put
this knowledge in their hearts. From the time the world was
created, people have seen the earth and sky and all that God
made. They can clearly see his invisible qualities—his eternal
power and divine nature. So they have no excuse whatsoever
for not knowing God.

Yes, they knew God, but they wouldn't worship him as
God or even give him thanks. And they began to think up
foolish ideas of what God was like. The result was that their
minds became dark and confused. Claiming to be wise, they
became utter fools instead. And instead of worshiping the glo-
rious, ever-living God, they worshiped idols made to look like
mere people, or birds and animals and snakes.

So God let them go ahead and do whatever shameful things
their hearts desired. As a result, they did vile and degrading
things with each other's bodies. Instead of believing what they
knew was the truth about God, they deliberately chose to
believe lies. So they worshiped the things God made but not
the Creator himself, who is to be praised forever.

ROMANS 1:18-25

The New Testament presents Jesus as the one who solves
the sin problem. The image used is the one of sacrifice,
based on the Old Testament idea of sacrificing an animal
as a "sin offering" to make peace with God. Jesus is the
final "offering," the one completely innocent person who let
himself be sacrificed to save sinners.

John saw Jesus coming toward him and said, "Look! There is
the Lamb of God who takes away the sin of the world!"

JOHN 1:29

God was in Christ, reconciling the world to himself, no longer counting people's sins against them. This is the wonderful message he has given us to tell others. God made Christ, who never sinned, to be the offering for our sin, so that we could be made right with God through Christ.

2 CORINTHIANS 5:19, 21

We are made right in God's sight when we trust in Jesus Christ to take away our sins. And we all can be saved in this same way, no matter who we are or what we have done.

For all have sinned; all fall short of God's glorious standard. Yet now God in his gracious kindness declares us not guilty. He has done this through Christ Jesus, who has freed us by taking away our sins. For God sent Jesus to take the punishment for our sins and to satisfy God's anger against us. We are made right with God when we believe that Jesus shed his blood, sacrificing his life for us.

ROMANS 3:22-25

He was handed over to die because of our sins, and he was raised from the dead to make us right with God.

ROMANS 4:25

When you were slaves of sin, you weren't concerned with doing what was right. And what was the result? It was not good, since now you are ashamed of the things you used to do, things that end in eternal doom. But now you are free from the power of sin and have become slaves of God. Now you do those things that lead to holiness and result in eternal life. For the wages of sin is death, but the free gift of God is eternal life through Christ Jesus our Lord.

ROMANS 6:20-23

See also Confessing Sin, Repentance, Salvation.

Success

Norman Vincent Peale defined success as "the development of a mature and constructive personality." This is certainly closer to the Bible's view than most people's. We usually define success in terms of money, power, influence—and being envied, of course. This is not the view of the Bible. In fact, the New Testament assures Jesus' followers that they may endure hardship, not success in the usual sense.

Don't let this discourage you. Our Lord did not tell us to give up all pleasure in this life. He merely told us that there were higher, better things—things that would last forever, and things that make worldly success seem trivial. Jesus proved this at the beginning of his earthly ministry, when Satan tempted him with worldly success.

> *Jesus was led out into the wilderness by the Holy Spirit to be tempted there by the Devil.*
>
> *The Devil took him to the peak of a very high mountain and showed him the nations of the world and all their glory. "I will give it all to you," he said, "if you will only kneel down and worship me."*
>
> *"Get out of here, Satan," Jesus told him. "For the Scriptures say, 'You must worship the Lord your God; serve only him.'"*
>
> MATTHEW 4:1, 8-10
>
> *Jesus answered, "I am not an earthly king. . . . My Kingdom is not of this world."*
>
> JOHN 18:36

How do you benefit if you gain the whole world but lose your own soul in the process? Is anything worth more than your soul?

MATTHEW 16:26

Those in frequent contact with the things of the world should make good use of them without becoming attached to them, for this world and all it contains will pass away.

1 CORINTHIANS 7:31

Don't copy the behavior and customs of this world, but let God transform you into a new person by changing the way you think. Then you will know what God wants you to do, and you will know how good and pleasing and perfect his will really is.

ROMANS 12:2

Where does this leave the philosophers, the scholars, and the world's brilliant debaters? God has made them all look foolish and has shown their wisdom to be useless nonsense.

Instead, God deliberately chose things the world considers foolish in order to shame those who think they are wise. And he chose those who are powerless to shame those who are powerful. God chose things despised by the world, things counted as nothing at all, and used them to bring to nothing what the world considers important, so that no one can ever boast in the presence of God.

1 CORINTHIANS 1:20, 27-29

God purchased you at a high price. Don't be enslaved by the world.

1 CORINTHIANS 7:23

God forbid that I should boast about anything except the cross of our Lord Jesus Christ. Because of that cross, my interest in this world died long ago, and the world's interest in me is also long dead. . . . What counts is whether we really have been changed into new and different people. May God's mercy and peace be upon all those who live by this principle. They are the new people of God.

GALATIANS 6:14-16

Tell those who are rich in this world not to be proud and not to trust in their money, which will soon be gone. But their trust should be in the living God, who richly gives us all we need for our enjoyment.

1 TIMOTHY 6:17

Don't you realize that friendship with this world makes you an enemy of God? I say it again, that if your aim is to enjoy this world, you can't be a friend of God.

JAMES 4:4

Stop loving this evil world and all that it offers you, for when you love the world, you show that you do not have the love of the Father in you. For the world offers only the lust for physical pleasure, the lust for everything we see, and pride in our possessions. These are not from the Father. They are from this evil world. And this world is fading away, along with everything it craves. But if you do the will of God, you will live forever.

1 JOHN 2:15-17

Those who love their life in this world will lose it. Those who despise their life in this world will keep it for eternal life.

JOHN 12:25

See also Work, Worry and Anxiety.

Temptation

A character in an Oscar Wilde play says, "I can resist everything except temptation." Following Wilde, the modern world doesn't take temptation too seriously. Listening to radio and TV, you might think the only temptations worth resisting are temptations to eat fat and cholesterol. (Is it because the only sin we can think of is overeating?)

But in fact, temptation *is* serious. Humans seem more inclined to do wrong than to do right. And everything around us says, "Go ahead, give in—everyone else is." We grow to accept the world's idea that the upright person is uptight, repressed, frustrated, and unhappy. But the Bible portrays temptation as serious—so serious that only God can give us what we need to resist it.

> *Wisdom will enter your heart, and knowledge will fill you with joy. Wise planning will watch over you. Understanding will keep you safe.*
>
> *Wisdom will save you from evil people, from those whose speech is corrupt.*
>
> PROVERBS 2:10-12

> *Sin is no longer your master, for you are no longer subject to the law, which enslaves you to sin. Instead, you are free by God's grace.*
>
> ROMANS 6:14

> *Humble yourselves before God. Resist the Devil, and he will flee from you.*
>
> JAMES 4:7

> *The Lord knows how to rescue godly people from their trials,*
> *even while punishing the wicked right up until the day of*
> *judgment.*
>
> 2 PETER 2:9

As these passages make clear, God himself is our rescuer.
It is never appropriate to ask why *God* is tempting us, for
God, as James explained, is never the source of anything
evil.

> *No one who wants to do wrong should ever say, "God is*
> *tempting me." God is never tempted to do wrong, and he*
> *never tempts anyone else either. Temptation comes from the*
> *lure of our own evil desires. These evil desires lead to evil*
> *actions, and evil actions lead to death. So don't be misled,*
> *my dear brothers and sisters.*
>
> *Whatever is good and perfect comes to us from God above,*
> *who created all heaven's lights. Unlike them, he never changes*
> *or casts shifting shadows.*
>
> JAMES 1:13-17

God allows us to be tempted. Why? Wouldn't it be better if
he just removed all temptation from our life? Easier, perhaps, but not better. Just as our muscles gain strength
from a physical workout—being stressed, tested—so we
gain spiritually from resisting temptation, as this passage
from James says so beautifully:

> *Dear brothers and sisters, whenever trouble comes your*
> *way, let it be an opportunity for joy. For when your faith is*
> *tested, your endurance has a chance to grow. So let it grow,*
> *for when your endurance is fully developed, you will be*
> *strong in character and ready for anything.*
>
> *God blesses the people who patiently endure testing. After-*

ward they will receive the crown of life that God has promised
to those who love him.

JAMES 1:2-4, 12

What about leading other people to sin? The legal system
calls it *soliciting* when someone tries to lead someone else
to commit a crime, and soliciting itself is a crime. The Bible
takes the same attitude toward people who deliberately
lead others to sin.

> Those who lead the upright into sin will fall into their own
> trap, but the honest will inherit good things.
>
> PROVERBS 28:10

> If anyone causes one of these little ones who trusts in me to
> lose faith, it would be better for that person to be thrown into
> the sea with a large millstone tied around the neck.
>
> MATTHEW 18:6

One of the joys of Christianity is that Jesus, its key figure,
is both God and human. While the faith is "spiritual," we
have the comfort of knowing that the founder of our faith is
a physical human being like us, someone who understands
our temptations because he has experienced them himself.

> Since he [Jesus] himself has gone through suffering and temp-
> tation, he is able to help us when we are being tempted.
>   This High Priest of ours understands our weaknesses, for he
> faced all of the same temptations we do, yet he did not sin.
>
> HEBREWS 2:18; 4:15

See also Self-Control and Self-Denial, Sin and Redemption.

The Tongue

This section could have been titled "Gossip" or "Slander" or "Criticism." Words can heal, but words can also do great harm. It doesn't require an outright lie to harm another person. A little insinuation, a hint, is often enough. Once a bit of "information" starts on the gossip grapevine, it rarely improves.

The Bible has much to say about our use—or abuse—of the tongue. We write gossip off as a relatively minor sin, but the Word of God takes a different view.

> *Do any of you want to live a life that is long and good? Then watch your tongue! Keep your lips from telling lies! Turn away from evil and do good. Work hard at living in peace with others.*
>
> *The eyes of the LORD watch over those who do right; his ears are open to their cries for help.*
>
> PSALM 34:12-15

> *Some people make cutting remarks, but the words of the wise bring healing.*
>
> PROVERBS 12:18

> *I will not tolerate people who slander their neighbors. I will not endure conceit and pride.*
>
> PSALM 101:5

> *As surely as a wind from the north brings rain, so a gossiping tongue causes anger!*
>
> PROVERBS 25:23

> *Fire goes out for lack of fuel, and quarrels disappear when gossip stops.*
>
> *A quarrelsome person starts fights as easily as hot embers light charcoal or fire lights wood.*
>
> PROVERBS 26:20-21

Jesus had much to say about the tongue. He was aware that people who are outwardly "religious" could abstain from the "big" sins like adultery and drunkenness. Yet these same people could do immense harm through their speech.

> *A tree is identified by its fruit. Make a tree good, and its fruit will be good. Make a tree bad, and its fruit will be bad. You brood of snakes! How could evil men like you speak what is good and right? For whatever is in your heart determines what you say. A good person produces good words from a good heart, and an evil person produces evil words from an evil heart. And I tell you this, that you must give an account on judgment day of every idle word you speak. The words you say now reflect your fate then; either you will be justified by them or you will be condemned.*
>
> MATTHEW 12:33-37

> *Evil words come from an evil heart and defile the person who says them. For from the heart come evil thoughts, murder, adultery, all other sexual immorality, theft, lying, and slander. These are what defile you.*
>
> MATTHEW 15:18-20

The classic passage on controlling the tongue is in James's letter. It ought to be posted on every Christian's bathroom mirror so that it could be read every morning.

*Those who control their tongues can also control themselves
in every other way. We can make a large horse turn around
and go wherever we want by means of a small bit in its
mouth. And a tiny rudder makes a huge ship turn wherever
the pilot wants it to go, even though the winds are strong. So
also, the tongue is a small thing, but what enormous damage
it can do. A tiny spark can set a great forest on fire. And the
tongue is a flame of fire. It is full of wickedness that can ruin
your whole life. It can turn the entire course of your life into
a blazing flame of destruction, for it is set on fire by hell
itself.*

*People can tame all kinds of animals and birds and reptiles
and fish, but no one can tame the tongue. It is an uncontrol-
lable evil, full of deadly poison. Sometimes it praises our Lord
and Father, and sometimes it breaks out into curses against
those who have been made in the image of God. And so blessing and cursing come pouring out of the same mouth. Surely,
my brothers and sisters, this is not right!*

JAMES 3:2-10

How much gossip and verbal cruelty goes under the name
of "constructive criticism"? In his letter James makes it
plain that criticizing fellow Christians—either to their face
or behind their back—is unchristian behavior.

*Don't speak evil against each other, my dear brothers and
sisters. If you criticize each other and condemn each other,
then you are criticizing and condemning God's law. But you
are not a judge who can decide whether the law is right or
wrong. Your job is to obey it. God alone, who made the law,
can rightly judge among us. He alone has the power to save
or to destroy. So what right do you have to condemn your
neighbor?*

JAMES 4:11-12

See also Anger, Hate, Judging Others.

Trusting God

Trust, like commitment, has become an evasive commodity in our world. People everywhere express a lack of trust in things they once considered dependable—government, schools, the media, even their own family members. So whom can we trust? The message of the Bible is clear: no one, except God. This doesn't mean we walk through the world feeling paranoid and suspicious. It means we hold a realistic view of human beings and institutions, not being too shocked when they fail us. It means we can feel secure anyway, knowing that God is faithful when no one else is.

> Trust in the LORD and do good. Then you will live safely in the land and prosper. Take delight in the LORD, and he will give you your heart's desires.
> Commit everything you do to the LORD. Trust him, and he will help you.
>
> PSALM 37:3-5

> God is our refuge and strength, always ready to help in times of trouble. So we will not fear, even if earthquakes come and the mountains crumble into the sea.
>
> PSALM 46:1-2

> The LORD God is our light and protector. He gives us grace and glory. No good thing will the LORD withhold from those who do what is right. O LORD Almighty, happy are those who trust in you.
>
> PSALM 84:11-12

Trust in the LORD with all your heart; do not depend on your own understanding. Seek his will in all you do, and he will direct your paths.

PROVERBS 3:5-6

Look at the proud! They trust in themselves, and their lives are crooked; but the righteous will live by their faith.

HABAKKUK 2:4

Why worry about your clothes? Look at the lilies and how they grow. They don't work or make their clothing, yet Solomon in all his glory was not dressed as beautifully as they are. And if God cares so wonderfully for flowers that are here today and gone tomorrow, won't he more surely care for you? You have so little faith!

So don't worry about having enough food or drink or clothing. Why be like the pagans who are so deeply concerned about these things? Your heavenly Father already knows all your needs, and he will give you all you need from day to day if you live for him and make the Kingdom of God your primary concern.

MATTHEW 6:28-33

Don't be afraid, little flock. For it gives your Father great happiness to give you the Kingdom.

LUKE 12:32

See also Faith, Hope.

Witnessing

Who would have thought, as this century drew to its close, how "evangelistic" people would become? People are evangelists—sometimes loud and violent ones—for animal rights, for abortion, against nuclear weapons, etc. Having a cause has become trendy.

In the Bible the only cause is the great Cause, God himself. The Bible has much to say about being a witness for this God and his goodness. Witnessing for God is sometimes confrontational, but it is never violent and never cruel.

> *How beautiful on the mountains are the feet of those who bring good news of peace and salvation, the news that the God of Israel reigns!*
>
> ISAIAH 52:7

> *The Spirit of the Sovereign LORD is upon me, because the LORD has appointed me to bring good news to the poor. He has sent me to comfort the brokenhearted and to announce that captives will be released and prisoners will be freed.*
>
> ISAIAH 61:1

> *You are the salt of the earth. But what good is salt if it has lost its flavor? Can you make it useful again? It will be thrown out and trampled underfoot as worthless. You are the light of the world—like a city on a mountain, glowing in the night for all to see. Don't hide your light under a basket! Instead, put it on a stand and let it shine for all. In the same way, let your good deeds shine out for all to see, so that everyone will praise your heavenly Father.*
>
> MATTHEW 5:13-16

The Good News about the Kingdom will be preached
throughout the whole world, so that all nations will hear it;
and then, finally, the end will come.

MATTHEW 24:14

When the Holy Spirit has come upon you, you will receive
power and will tell people about me everywhere—in Jerusa-
lem, throughout Judea, in Samaria, and to the ends of the
earth.

ACTS 1:8

After the Gospels the New Testament could be called the
"Book of Witnesses," as the story unfolds of the apostles
and their witnessing about the good news of Christ. Witnessing often brought persecution, but Jesus' followers
knew they could not keep the Good News to themselves,
no matter what the world might think or do.

You are to take his message everywhere, telling the whole
world what you have seen and heard.

ACTS 22:15

God was in Christ, reconciling the world to himself, no
longer counting people's sins against them. This is the won-
derful message he has given us to tell others. We are Christ's
ambassadors, and God is using us to speak to you. We urge
you, as though Christ himself were here pleading with you,
"Be reconciled to God!"

2 CORINTHIANS 5:19-20

Whatever you do or say, let it be as a representative of the
Lord Jesus, all the while giving thanks through him to God
the Father.

COLOSSIANS 3:17

Live wisely among those who are not Christians, and make the most of every opportunity. Let your conversation be gracious and effective so that you will have the right answer for everyone.

COLOSSIANS 4:5-6

God has not given us a spirit of fear and timidity, but of power, love, and self-discipline. So you must never be ashamed to tell others about our Lord. And don't be ashamed of me, either, even though I'm in prison for Christ. With the strength God gives you, be ready to suffer with me for the proclamation of the Good News.

2 TIMOTHY 1:7-8

Work

Work has become a four-letter word for many people. Societies go through cycles—one generation works hard and plays little, another generation reverses the trend. Right now we seem to be in a pro-play, antiwork attitude. We seem to have forgotten the truth of William James's statement: "Nothing is work unless you would rather be doing something else." In other words, if you truly enjoy work, it isn't work. Maybe we've neglected this truth and fallen prey to the "can't wait till Friday" mentality. The Bible makes no pleasant promises to people who spend their entire workweek looking forward to the weekend.

> *Hard work means prosperity; only fools idle away their time.*
>   *Work hard and become a leader; be lazy and become a slave.*
>   *Lazy people don't even cook the game they catch, but the diligent make use of everything they find.*
>   PROVERBS 12:11, 24, 27

> *An empty stable stays clean, but no income comes from an empty stable.*
>   *Work brings profit, but mere talk leads to poverty!*
>   PROVERBS 14:4, 23

To balance out the "work-hard-and-succeed" promises of the book of Proverbs, the book of Ecclesiastes assures us that human beings cannot find their *ultimate* satisfaction in work. Only God can provide that kind of satisfaction.

> *As I looked at everything I had worked so hard to accomplish, it was all so meaningless. It was like chasing the wind. There was nothing really worthwhile anywhere.*
>
> ECCLESIASTES 2:11

Paul, a hard worker in the Lord's service, had no patience with laziness. He knew that idleness not only displeased God but also gave unbelievers a low opinion of Christians.

> *This should be your ambition: to live a quiet life, minding your own business and working with your hands, just as we commanded you before. As a result, people who are not Christians will respect the way you live, and you will not need to depend on others to meet your financial needs.*
>
> 1 THESSALONIANS 4:11-12

> *Those who won't care for their own relatives, especially those living in the same household, have denied what we believe. Such people are worse than unbelievers.*
>
> 1 TIMOTHY 5:8

Paul promised Christians something that we often forget: work does not need to be humdrum, because we can do it to the glory of God. Like any part of ourselves, our work—whatever it may be—can honor the Lord.

> *Work hard, but not just to please your masters when they are watching. As slaves of Christ, do the will of God with all your heart. Work with enthusiasm, as though you were working for the Lord rather than for people.*
>
> EPHESIANS 6:6-7

See also Money, Success.

Worry and Anxiety

Christian author William R. Inge defined worry as "interest paid on trouble before it becomes due." Worry is the great plague of life, both for believers and unbelievers. It crosses all educational, economic, and racial boundaries. It is human to worry, to fret, to fear the future.

Worry may be normal, but it also sinful. "Sinful?" you say. Definitely. The Bible is brimming over with promises to God's people. So we need *not* worry, for it is God—not we—who is in control of the universe.

> Happy are those who fear the LORD. Yes, happy are those who delight in doing what he commands. . . . When darkness overtakes the godly, light will come bursting in. They are generous, compassionate, and righteous. All goes well for those who are generous, who lend freely and conduct their business fairly. Such people will not be overcome by evil circumstances. Those who are righteous will be long remembered. They do not fear bad news; they confidently trust the LORD to care for them. They are confident and fearless and can face their foes triumphantly.
>
> PSALM 112:1-8

> Give your burdens to the LORD, and he will take care of you. He will not permit the godly to slip and fall.
>
> PSALM 55:22

> As pressure and stress bear down on me, I find joy in your commands.
>
> PSALM 119:143

Worry weighs a person down; an encouraging word cheers a person up.

PROVERBS 12:25

Jesus himself, the Son of God, spoke many times on the subject of worry. Jesus showed that he completely depended on his Father, and he promised his followers that they, too, could—and should—devote their lives to something more fruitful than worrying.

I tell you, don't worry about everyday life—whether you have enough food, drink, and clothes. Doesn't life consist of more than food and clothing? Look at the birds. They don't need to plant or harvest or put food in barns because your heavenly Father feeds them. And you are far more valuable to him than they are. Can all your worries add a single moment to your life? Of course not.

And why worry about your clothes? Look at the lilies and how they grow. They don't work or make their clothing, yet Solomon in all his glory was not dressed as beautifully as they are. And if God cares so wonderfully for flowers that are here today and gone tomorrow, won't he more surely care for you? You have so little faith!

So don't worry about having enough food or drink or clothing. Why be like the pagans who are so deeply concerned about these things? Your heavenly Father already knows all your needs, and he will give you all you need from day to day if you live for him and make the Kingdom of God your primary concern.

So don't worry about tomorrow, for tomorrow will bring its own worries. Today's trouble is enough for today.

MATTHEW 6:25-34

The apostle Paul, in the following passage, promised Christians that they can dispel worry by fixing their minds on good things, not on their worries. It is one of the classic Bible passages on worry, one that people should engrave on their hearts.

Don't worry about anything; instead, pray about everything. Tell God what you need, and thank him for all he has done. If you do this, you will experience God's peace, which is far more wonderful than the human mind can understand. His peace will guard your hearts and minds as you live in Christ Jesus.

And now, dear brothers and sisters, let me say one more thing as I close this letter. Fix your thoughts on what is true and honorable and right. Think about things that are pure and lovely and admirable. Think about things that are excellent and worthy of praise.

PHILIPPIANS 4:6-8

See also Contentment, Joy, Peace, Trusting God.